Introductory Psychology:
History, Themes and Perspectives

Crucial Study Texts for Psychology Degree Courses

Titles in series

Clinical Psychology	ISBN: 1 903337 20 8	Price £12.00
Cognitive Psychology	ISBN: 1 903337 13 5	Price £12.00
Developmental Psychology	ISBN: 1 903337 14 3	Price £12.00
Introductory Psychology: History Themes and Perspectives	ISBN: 1 903337 17 8	Price £12.00
Research Methods and Statistics	ISBN: 1 903337 15 1	Price £9.99

To order, please call our order line 0845 230 9000, or email orders@learningmatters.co.uk, or visit our website www.learningmatters.co.uk

Introductory Psychology: History, Themes and Perspectives

Meg Barker

Psychology series editor:
Eamon Fulcher

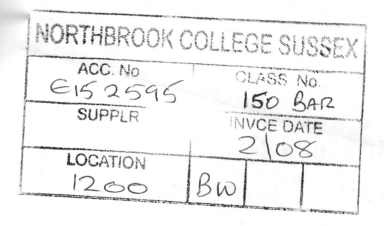
First published in 2003 by Crucial, a division of Learning Matters Ltd.

British Library Cataloguing in Publication Data
A CIP record for this book is available from the British Library.

ISBN 1 903337 17 8

Cover design by Topics – The Creative Partnership
Project management by Deer Park Productions
Text design by Code 5 Design
Typeset by PDQ Typesetting, Newcastle under Lyme
Printed and bound by Bell & Bain Ltd, Glasgow

Learning Matters Ltd
33 Southernhay East
Exeter EX1 1NX
Tel: 01392 215560
Email: info@learningmatters.co.uk
www.learningmatters.co.uk

Contents

Foreword

This book is for anyone who wants to learn about psychology. My aim in writing it was to provide an interesting and accessible introduction to the history of psychology, the different branches in psychology and the main issues that psychologists debate. So hopefully you will enjoy and understand everything in this book even if you've never read anything about psychology before. I've tried to include all the really vital things to know about psychology, with lots of examples to help you understand the trickier bits. If you have done some psychology before, perhaps an A level or an access course, this book should help you to fit everything you've learnt together, to see how psychology works as a discipline and to build on your existing knowledge. I've also incorporated some of the issues and areas that I find most fascinating, and that students I teach are always keen to know more about.

Although I hope the book will be of interest to any reader, it is specifically aimed at people on undergraduate degrees. The book is designed to get you through an introductory course in psychology, giving you the knowledge you need about psychology, and also the skills you'll need to pass the assessments.

You might be taking a whole degree in psychology, in which case the material in this book will be helpful as a general foundation and will also give you some ideas about what you might be able to do after your degree (see section 3 of Chapter 3). Alternatively you might be doing a degree in something other than psychology and just be taking a few psychology courses as a minor or subsidiary subject. If this is the case, you may well be a bit anxious that you don't know quite how to 'do' psychology. This book will make that very clear, and will give you the knowledge needed for an introductory psychology course. If you read this book and do all the suggested exercises and sample questions you should be very well equipped to write essays, give presentations and take exams on such a course.

The introduction to the book gives general advice about studying and passing assessments in psychology. The rest of the book gives you information about history, theories and perspectives in psychology. Most of the basics are covered here, but each chapter also gives you references to good, accessible books that cover the various areas in more detail. These references will be particularly helpful to follow up if you have an essay or presentation to do in that area.

I want this book to be as useful as possible to you the reader. If you spot any errors as you read it, or come across any parts that you find difficult to understand, please let me know. My e-mail address is m.barker@worc.ac.uk. Do also let me know if you have any positive comments!

I would like to thank those who have helped me to bring this book into being: Eamon Fulcher, the series editor, and Jonathan Harris and Mandy Preece from Learning Matters.

This book is dedicated to the people who've shaped who I am as a person and as a psychologist:

- My family, Nick Pearson-Woodd, Darren Oldridge, and Ani Ritchie;
- Dave Clarke, Dai Jones and Jonathan Elcock.

Introduction
Study and revision skills for psychology

Chapter summary

This introduction is about studying psychology in higher education. It covers student life in general and gives tips about how to learn about psychology effectively. Perhaps most importantly, this chapter provides advice about how to pass the different types of assessment that you will encounter on a psychology course. The chapter focuses on the skills needed for introductory psychology courses, but these apply to most of the other courses you will do on a psychology degree (whether you are taking it as your main/major subject or as a minor/subsidiary subject).

The one type of assessment not covered in this chapter is the research report. That is because this is covered in depth in the Crucial Study Text on research methods and statistics. If your main/major degree is psychology, you will find that book a very helpful companion to this one since research projects will be a vital part of your course.

Section 1

Doing psychology in higher education

The aims of this book and this chapter

As you will see if you read the Foreword this book aims to give you the following:

- an interesting and accessible introduction to the topic of psychology;
- the knowledge needed to get through an introductory psychology course;
- the skills needed to pass the assessments on such a course;
- an overall foundation in psychology to set you up for the rest of your psychology courses/modules.

The rest of the book covers the content of psychology: the history of the discipline, the main approaches to studying psychology, the topics covered in psychology, and debates about psychological research and theory.

This chapter focuses on skills. It covers the abilities you need to undertake a psychology course in higher education. These are:

- minimising stress, so that you can work well;
- managing your time successfully;
- learning from lectures, seminars and the written materials that you read;
- writing essays, presentations and exam answers.

In this first section, we will cover the first two of these. It's vital to get these basics in place because otherwise it will be difficult to work well, however skilled you are at taking notes or writing essays. Psychologists have found that people work badly when they are stressed: they find it hard to concentrate and to remember things. Ensuring that you have a healthy, low-stress environment where you feel in control of your time and supported by other people is an important foundation to doing well in higher education.

Minimising stress

Since I finished my psychology degree back in 1995, I've done a lot of research on student life and have talked to hundreds of students about their experiences. The advice here is based on what they have found to work best, but not all these strategies work for everybody. Consider what has worked for you in the past and try out some of the additional suggestions made here.

Tips for minimising stress:

- Be prepared before you start higher education. Many students who have problems say it's because they didn't do what was right for them, or they had unrealistic expectations. Find out as much as you can about the institution, your course (by reading books like this one) and what it's like being a student (by talking to existing students).

- Don't feel pressurised by the common idea that student days are 'the best days of your life'. Realistically, there will be good bits and bad bits, and the transition to higher education can be tough due to all the adjustments you're making (often to a new environment, living situation, social group, way of working and financial situation). Remember that everyone is in the same boat and it's natural to feel a bit stressed and overwhelmed at times.

- If you do get into difficulties, get support as soon as possible. There are people at your institution to help with any problem (e.g. tutors, student union, counsellors, financial advisors). Find the appropriate person and approach them. Remember they are paid to help you and will probably have been through similar things when they were a student. Sometimes the first person you go to isn't very friendly or helpful. Keep trying till you find someone who is.

- Build up a support network. Talk to other students you come across in the first few days in accommodation, lectures and queues. Find out where they're from and what they're doing. They'll be relieved that someone spoke to them. Join a few societies about things you're into. Go to social events that appeal to you. There are often groups for mature students, international students, Christian students, lesbian/gay/ bisexual students, etc.

- Have a budget. Figure out in advance how much money you have available per month and per week and allocate it to the different things you need (accommodation, bills, food, phone, social life, textbooks, etc.). Note down everything you spend each week under each category to keep track of it.

- Make sure you have somewhere private to work, at least at certain times, with all the stuff you need and a 'do not disturb' sign. The library can be a great place to work if you lack privacy. Allocate time to spend there.

Time management

Students find time management difficult whether they've come straight from school or have worked for years. It's hard to get a balance and give enough time to everything in your life. Most students have to juggle their academic work and social life. Many also have to factor in part-time work, family and other interests. You'll be taking several courses, all with different demands on your time. Lecturers and tutors won't chase you for assignments, so you have to get things in on time, otherwise you'll fail. There are many distractions from work, so it can be hard to motivate yourself.

It's easy to neglect your studies with all the exciting prospects of student life. However, it's equally easy to get too involved with work and not give yourself vital time for relaxation, sleep, exercise and seeing friends. Here are some tips that may help you to strike the right balance. You don't have to follow them all rigidly, but you may find some useful.

- **Timetable.** Once you have all the course programmes, make up a timetable of your week so you can see how all the lectures, seminars, etc. fit together. Include regular sports/clubs. Schedule in time to spend on academic work and part-time jobs. Think about which time of day you find it easiest to work (this varies from person to person). Schedule in time to relax too. Have at least one day a week completely off, and other free time too. A blank timetable to fill in is given on p. 4.

- **Diary.** It's good to put this information in a weekly diary, so you can add in the stuff that varies by week. Some people like one they can carry round; some prefer a big wall chart so they can see the whole term at a glance. Write assessment deadlines in with brightly coloured pen so you can see them coming. Then write in reminder notes, e.g.

  - three weeks before 'start preparing and researching essay for course X';
  - two weeks before 'have all the material collected for course X essay, write essay plan';
  - one week before 'write rough draft of essay for course X';
  - four days before 'write final version of essay for course X, read over, check spelling, get a friend to read over'.

  This way, deadlines can't just sneak up on you. Also write in all your lectures, seminars and preparation for these. Spread work over the term evenly rather than having some weeks when you do nothing and some when you try to do it all. This may mean doing an essay that's due in week 8 in week 4. That's OK. You can always go back to it in week 8 and add extra stuff, but at least you've done it.

- **Break things down.** If you're feeling overwhelmed by work, write a list of what you actually have to do to get things in perspective. Break things into smaller, manageable tasks. For example, writing an essay sounds scary, so break it down into: go to the library to search for books and journals, read a chapter to get an overview of the topic, read a couple more things underlining the important points, write a structure for the essay, write the introduction, write section 1, 2, 3, write the conclusion, check through essay. Give yourself rewards for completing each task, such as a TV programme, a cup of coffee, a phone call or going out with a friend.

- **Prioritise.** Mark tasks according to urgency to see what needs doing first. However, we all have times when we haven't got the energy or concentration for writing. If you have a list, you can decide to use that time for something else you have to do, like going to the library or discussing work with a friend. Working with others often doesn't seem like such hard work and you motivate each other.

- **Be effective.** Sitting and staring at a book you don't understand for hours is ineffective. Find a simpler book that you do understand, read and summarise that, then go on to more complex material. Getting stressed about an essay is ineffective. Chat with someone else on your course and/or your tutor about it. This will calm you

weekly timetable

DAY	8–9	9–10	10–11	11–12	12–13	13–14	14–15	15–16	16–17	17–18	18–19	19–20
Mon												
Tues												
Wed												
Thurs												
Fri												
Sat												
Sun												

down and get it clearer in your head. Take time out and come back to it when you feel fresher. Have regular breaks from work. People can't concentrate for more than 40 minutes continuously.

─── CRUCIAL TIP ───

You won't get all this right immediately. Don't get angry with yourself if you make some mistakes initially. Just try to learn from them for next time.

Section 2

Learning about psychology

Learning from lectures and seminars

One of the first things that will strike you about your course is how few lectures there actually are, especially if you're comparing it to A level courses at school/college. This is why it's so important to manage the rest of your time; you're expected to do a lot of learning outside of taught sessions.

Here are some ways of ensuring that you get the most out of lectures and seminars:

- Get any information available before the session (e.g. notes from web, readings). Think up questions you want answered in the session.

- Write notes during the session. Don't try to write down everything. Focus on key points and overall structure. If a lecturer goes too fast ask them to put the basics on the web or a handout.

- Go over your notes as soon as possible after the session. Either write them up or highlight important bits. Add information from the course text and look up anything you didn't understand.

- Think about how this session fits in with the rest of the course, particularly any assessments. Keep the notes and papers from each course together in a file.

─── CRUCIAL TIP ───

Get to know another student on each course so you can take notes for each other if you miss sessions. You can work on group assignments and revise together, as well as meeting socially after sessions to chat about them.

Learning from books

You'll get long book lists for all your courses. These can be quite intimidating, so the first thing to know is that you're not expected to read all the books on the list! Neither are those the only books that could be useful.

There'll be one or two 'course', 'core' or 'main' texts. These are the ones worth getting hold of. Don't buy them straightaway though; academic textbooks can be really expensive. Go to the library or bookshop early on, find out which book is on your wavelength and suited to your ability. Don't get a difficult one; it'll just make you feel bad. You can always build up from a more basic book.

That said, be wary of using books designed for a level below yours (e.g. A level or access course). Tutors won't be impressed if you reference these, so read some undergraduate books too. In the first year, introductory texts like this one are appropriate but as you go through the degree you'll need to specialise more.

The other books on the book list are for reference if you are doing an assessment on that topic. You rarely need to read a whole book, often just one chapter or section. When revising for short answer or multiple-choice exams, lecture notes and main textbooks are usually enough.

If you do buy your own books, write in them as you read: highlighting, making notes in the margins and marking key pages. You can sometimes get books second-hand from noticeboards, student bookshops and websites like Amazon.

Learning from journal articles

Psychology students are also expected to use journal articles in their assessments, especially in the second and third year. Your library will have a range of psychological journals. Go and look through them to see what's there. Journals can be daunting when you're not used to them. Most are pretty specialised. *The Psychologist* is a general journal that aims to be readable for students. It's worth looking at this each month to keep up with what's going on in psychology.

Other than this, you'll use journal articles for specific assignments. Looking through the journals is time consuming, so do a computer search. The librarians will tell you how this is done. Generally it involves using a CD-Rom (like 'psychlit') or web-based journal search (like the *Web of Science*). You type in key words and print off abstracts of articles that are relevant.

CRUCIAL TIP

An abstract is the summary of a journal article that is printed at the start of the article.

The key words you use are important. Sometimes you'll type in a word (e.g. 'emotion') and get thousands of articles. If this happens, focus your search (e.g. 'emotional Stroop task' – see Chapter 3). However, being too specific may give no articles at all. In this case, you need to broaden out. Think about all the words related to the topic you're after and try different combinations. The help menus and librarians can aid you in conducting your searches.

Once you've printed off the abstracts, find out whether your library carries the journals they're from. If so, photocopy the whole article. If not, order it through Inter-Library Loan (ask the librarians how to do this).

Learning from Internet resources

These days there are many psychological resources on the Internet. Several journals publish their articles on the web. However, the quality of web material varies greatly. For example, if you type the word 'personality' into a search engine like 'Yahoo!' or 'Google' you get everything from academic articles and lecture notes on personality, to encyclopaedia definitions, personal opinion websites, and personality quizzes based on the characters from Winnie The Pooh! Usually material from a university or other academic organisation/ journal is OK, but be wary of including anything from personal home pages or news sites; such material can be biased and is rarely referenced properly.

Survey

Skim the text to get an overview of the chapter or article.
- Read the abstract or summary at the start/end.
- Look over the subheadings.
- Look at any figures, diagrams, tables or graphs.
- Read the introductory and concluding paragraphs.

Question

Take one short section at a time (the introduction, method, results and discussion in an article or the sub-sections of a chapter). For each one, before you read it, ask yourself:
- What is it going to tell you? What are you going to learn from reading it?
- What was the author aiming to do in that section?
- How does it relate to what you already know?

Read

Read the section you have been questioning.
- Keep your questions in mind as you read.
- Don't make notes at this stage.
- Try to integrate what you read with what you already know.

Recall

- Make notes on what you have learnt from the section.
- Recall the important parts of the section you read and note them down.
- Don't copy from the text, summarise in note form.
  This aids understanding.
- If you can't remember something, read it again, then write notes when you've finished reading.

Review

Review what you have learnt (at the end of each section, and once you've read the whole chapter or article).
- Test yourself to make sure you've understood.
- Answer any test questions that the author has included, or make some up yourself.
- Write a brief overall summary of the key points in the chapter or article.

The SQ3R technique

Using books, articles and other resources: the SQ3R technique

So what do you do once you've got a bunch of appropriate books, journal articles and web resources? Don't sit down and read them through from start to finish. It might feel like you've done a lot of work, but really you'll have taken very little in because your brain will have skipped bits and switched off in places. Instead, keep the assessment question in mind as you read and focus on what is directly relevant to that. Use contents pages and indexes and skim chapters to find the right bits. Most authors recommend the SQ3R technique to get the most out of reading. See the diagram on page 7 for how to do this.

It is also useful to do the following:

- Keep a psychology dictionary handy (such as Hayes and Stratton, 1999). Jot down what words mean;
- Write in full useful direct quotations, with full reference (see section 3);
- Use flow diagrams, spider diagrams, mind maps, tables, bullet points etc. in note-taking – anything that makes notes clear and easy to understand. Use your own abbreviations in notes to speed up writing. Some I find useful are:

Ψ	psychology	↑	increase
Ψ^t	psychologist	↓	decrease
em^n	emotion	∴	therefore (or upside-down for because)
em^{nl}	emotional	&	and
$diff^t$	different	w/	with
?	question	w/o	without.

Section 3

Writing about psychology

Writing essays

At the end of each chapter of this book there are a number of questions that could be set on the topics covered in the chapter. For each one I've said what answers should cover. This section gives general advice on writing psychology essays. Refer back to it as you consider the questions in the text.

Essays are one of the main assessment methods used in psychology, so it's vital to know how to write them. There are some general writing skills to follow, such as clear wording, appropriate punctuation and well-structured paragraphs. Also, there are some things that psychology tutors in particular look for. This may differ from what's expected on other degree programmes like English or history. It's important to tailor your essay to the subject. For example, in psychology, you can use tables and diagrams, and a clear structure is very important.

The advice in this section generally refers to coursework essays, but most of the points also apply to exam essays. Exams in general will be covered later. The points about writing and structure also apply to research reports, which are covered in depth in the Crucial Study Text on research methods and statistics.

Below are seven golden rules for writing psychology essays. They come from my experience of what students struggle with. It's also helpful to look at example essays that have obtained good grades in the past. You may be able to get these from your tutors.

Rule 1: Check your English, grammar, spelling and presentation

The person reading your essay needs to easily understand what you are saying. They won't be able to do this if there are lots of spelling mistakes and grammatical errors. If you're concerned about your general writing ability, many institutions put on essay-skills classes and some useful books are mentioned at the end of this chapter. Mature students often worry about this if they haven't written an essay for several years. Most institutions provide extra support for dyslexic students and students for whom English is not their first language. There may be classes, people to read over assessments, help in exams or other support, depending on your institution.

One of the most common problems in student essays is the over-long sentence or paragraph. If in doubt, stick to short sentences, and have at least three paragraphs to a page. Look at books to see how they divide up sentences and paragraphs and emulate this.

We generally don't use the first person (I or we) in psychology essays. Instead of saying 'I am going to write about X and Y', you should say 'this essay will address X and Y'. Instead of saying 'I think that W', you should say 'it seems that W' or 'the research suggests that W' (and give references to support this – see later).

Spell checkers are great, but they only pick up misspellings that aren't real words. I'll never forget the student who referred to Freud as 'Fraud' throughout the whole of their essay!

Present your essay clearly. Follow any advice given in the course outline. Generally work needs to be typed (or very neatly handwritten). Avoid using a very big or very small font; 10 point Times is generally good. Have 1.5 spacing and margins so the marker can write comments there. Number your pages. Use a folder that makes life easy for the marker; avoid presenting work in heavy files or ones where each page is in a separate envelope.

Rule 2: Have a good, clear structure

Your essay needs an introduction, a main body and a conclusion. The rule of thumb is 'tell your reader what you're going to tell them, tell them it, and then tell them what you've told them'! The introduction and conclusion shouldn't be too long, about 100–200 words or half a side is usually about right for a 2,000 word essay. The introduction should clearly state how you are going to answer the question, giving the reader a feel for the area and the structure of the essay that is to follow. For example, a good introduction to the essay 'evaluate the main theories of language acquisition' would be:

> The two contrasting views on the way in which children acquire language are those of nativism and empiricism. The extremes of these two approaches are, respectively, that language is entirely learnt through experience and that language is completely innate.

> It seems fairly obvious that both these extremes are untenable. The important question to address is to what extent language is learnt or innate, since it is probable that both these factors are involved in language acquisition. In addressing this question, the work of various nativists and empiricists needs to be examined to establish the strengths and weaknesses of the two positions.

> This essay will evaluate the views of the main empiricist and nativist theorists, Skinner and Chomsky, before going on to consider more interactionist positions.

> (See section 3 of Chapter 5 for more information on this topic.)

This sets out the area and key positions and clearly outlines the structure of the essay so the reader knows exactly where it's going.

The main body of the essay should be clearly structured into different sections, whether these are given subheadings or not. When planning your essay, think carefully about this structure. For example, in the language acquisition essay I would have three subsections: Skinner's theory, Chomsky's position and the interactionist perspectives. Within each section I would have various points to make. A very helpful rule is that each paragraph should make one separate point. The first sentence of the paragraph should make the point, and the rest of the paragraph should support it with more information, examples and/or evidence. For example, in the 'Skinner' section of this essay, I might have a paragraph outlining Skinner's general position, one summarising his theory of language acquisition and one putting forward the objections other people have raised with this theory. Then the first paragraph of my 'Chomsky' section would begin with his criticisms of Skinner's ideas.

CRUCIAL TIP

Assume that all psychology essay questions ask for the answer to make reference to specific psychological examples, even if they don't actually say that.

It's also helpful to include regular signposts for the reader, particularly in a long essay. At the end of each section, take a couple of sentences to summarise briefly what you've said in that section, what you are going onto next and why, clarifying how this relates to the question set.

Towards the end of the essay you need to give a synthesis, drawing together all the points that have been made. This should be followed by your conclusion, which should sum up your argument. It should not just repeat the introduction, nor should it introduce any new material.

Rule 3: Keep wording simple

Students often use overcomplicated wording in psychology essays because they want to come across as 'academic'. Actually, this often gets in the way of the reader's under-standing. Never use a word or phrase you don't properly understand yourself. Avoid using long, complicated words when shorter ones will do. The first thing the marker assesses is whether you've understood the area. They can't do this unless the wording is clear and understandable. If in doubt, use the KIS rule: Keep It Simple. Explain everything as clearly as possible. It often helps to imagine the person reading the essay. You should write so that one of you fellow students on the psychology course, who is not themselves writing an essay on this topic, could understand it. Be careful not to assume any knowledge of the area on the part of the reader, other than a basic understanding of psychology. Explain everything fully, giving examples to illustrate if possible.

Students often get 'wordy', using long, repetitive sentences. Keep sentences short and to the point. For example, the following sentence is very wordy: 'There were all sorts of problems in relation to the way in which the study was carried out that meant the results might not be seen as very reliable.' This could be better written as: 'The reliability of the study can be questioned due to the following problems with the way it was conducted' (and then go on to say what those were).

Rule 4: Use diagrams, tables or graphs if appropriate

A picture can be worth a thousand words. For example, Figure 5.5 in Chapter 5 would be appropriate to include in the essay on language acquisition mentioned above.

Rule 5: Read the question; answer the question

It's extremely important to answer the question set. Students often make the mistake of writing a general essay on the topic, rather than answering the specific question. For example, for the question 'can personality best be explained by nature or nurture?' a poor answer would cover what personality is and outline various theories of personality, rather than evaluating the nature/nurture explanations. Unpack the question in your introduction saying how you understand it and how you are going to answer it. This is particularly important if it is quite a complex question. Stay relevant to the question throughout the essay, making clear to the reader how what you are saying relates to it. Address your first and last paragraphs explicitly to the question title.

CRUCIAL TIP

Always put yourself in the reader's shoes when writing an essay or exam answer. Be clear what you are saying and why you are saying it, in relation to the question.

Rule 6: Know how you will be assessed

Find out from your tutors the criteria on which the essay will be assessed. For example, places where I've taught have had summary tables of what is required for each grade: what a student has to demonstrate to get a 3rd, 2:2, 2:1, etc. Use the assessment criteria to plan, write and check your essay and make sure you've met them all. There may even be a checklist that the tutors use when marking essays. Refer to this as you write them.

Sometimes tutors have slight differences in what they like in essays. For example, some like you to use subheadings and some do not (although you should always write in subsections, whether you label them or not). Check out with tutors anything they particularly look for, or any 'pet hates' they have. Small things like this shouldn't make a difference to your grade since all tutors mark to the same criteria, but it's always worth keeping your marker in a good mood!

Rule 7: Plan your answer first; check it through afterwards

Spend a lot of time planning the essay before you start writing it. Many students find 'mind maps' a helpful starting point. Write the essay topic in the middle of a sheet of paper and then write around it all the relevant theories and studies you need to mention, drawing lines to represent links. Add to this as you read about the subject.

When writing the essay, don't start at the beginning and just write through to the end. Plan the essay structure first. Write the overall structure (introduction, subsections, conclusion), then write one sentence for each paragraph within each section which summarises the main point you want to make in that paragraph. Make sure the points flow well from one to the next. Then start filling in the details. Writing an essay this way is also less daunting than writing it straight through because it breaks it into manageable chunks.

Once you've finished the essay, check it through carefully. Reading it out aloud can help a lot. Ask yourself the following questions:

- Does each sentence make sense? (KIS)
- Does each paragraph make a point and support it?
- Does the structure flow with each paragraph following from the last?
- Is there a clear introduction and conclusion?
- Is every paragraph clearly relevant to the question?
- Are all statements properly referenced?
- Are all the references included in the reference list?

Get a friend to read through your work because it is hard to spot errors in something you've written yourself. Give them this checklist and ask them to be brutally honest! They can tell you anything they didn't completely understand and you can clarify those places.

One of the most important things in psychology essays is correct referencing, so this is covered in a separate section, below.

Referencing

Your department will have guidelines on how to reference. Get hold of these and follow them. The advice here is the general psychology way of doing things, but your department may differ slightly in its advice, so check this.

You need to provide references throughout your essay to acknowledge ideas or research findings from other people's work. Always substantiate your claims by providing references to support what you are saying.

Most psychology departments use the APA (American Psychological Association) form of referencing, where the author and date of the work is included in the text (rather than using footnotes or numbered references). There are two ways in which you can put the name and date in the text, shown below:

Pennebaker (1997) found that expressing emotions was good for people's health.

Or

Expressing emotions has been found to be good for people's health (Pennebaker, 1997).

The only information you should give is the author's surname and the date of their work. Don't give book names or initials of authors.

If there are two authors, give both their names (e.g. Jones and Elcock, 2001). If there are more than two authors, give all the authors' names the first time you mention them (e.g. Haney, Banks and Zimbardo, 1973), but after that you can use 'et al.' rather than giving all the names each time (e.g. Haney et al., 1973).

If you are quoting someone directly, you need to give the page number of the quote. For example:

Pennebaker (1997) states that 'confronting our deepest thoughts and feelings can have remarkable short- and long-term health benefits' (p.2).

Or just

'Confronting our deepest thoughts and feelings can have remarkable short- and long-term health benefits.' (Pennebaker, 1997, p. 2).

Don't use too many quotes in your essay. Generally it is better to paraphrase what people have said because that shows you've understood it. Don't quote authors of general textbooks. Quotes should be from authors of original theories or studies, and should be used when it's important to give the exact wording of what they said.

Paraphrasing is using different wording to explain something someone else has said. This demonstrates that you've understood it fully and also protects you from accusations of plagiarism. Plagiarism is copying what someone else has written without referencing it properly, or copying another student's work. Be very careful about this because tutors can recognise changes in style when someone has copied something from a book, essay or website. There are very tough penalties for plagiarism. Even when you paraphrase, make sure you reference the source of the information.

Reference the original author, not just the book you got the information from. For example, imagine you are writing an essay on Freud and have been reading about Freud's theories in Michael Eysenck's *Psychology Student's Handbook*. The book tells you that Freud (1915) said that repression was a defence mechanism that kept disturbing thoughts out of the conscious mind. If you want to say this in your essay, you should reference it to Freud (1915), not to

Eysenck (2000), since it was Freud who said it originally. You mention where the reference comes from in the reference list (see information on 'secondary references' below).

Every reference used should be included in the reference list at the end of the essay. Students often get confused about reference lists and bibliographies. A bibliography is a list of books you've read whereas a reference list is a list of all the references mentioned in the essay. Most psychology departments require that essays have a reference list but not a bibliography.

The reference list should include all the references cited in the essay. That means there shouldn't be any references on the list you haven't mentioned in the body of the essay (for example, a book that you read but didn't cite). Also, there shouldn't be any references in the essay that are not included in the reference list. Compile the reference list as you write the essay. Each time you mention someone, put their full reference in the reference list. The list should be in alphabetical order of author surnames.

The reference list at the end of this book gives you plenty of examples of how to write references. Here are the basic formats with examples:

Books:
Author(s) (date) *Title of Book.* Place of publication: Publisher. For example:

> Pennebaker, J. W. (1997) *Opening Up: The Healing Power of Expressing Emotions.* London: The Guilford Press.

Chapters in edited books:
Author(s) (date) 'Title of article', in editor(s) (eds), *Title of Book.* Place of publication: Publisher. For example:

> Stevens, R. (1995) 'Freudian theories of personality', in S. E. Hampson and A. M. Colman (eds), *Individual Differences and Personality.* London: Longman.

Journal articles:
Author(s) (date) 'Title of article', *Name of Journal*, volume (issue if available), pages. For example:

> Lea, Stephen E. F. (2000) 'Towards an ethical use of animals', *The Psychologist*, 13 (11): 556–7.

Internet
For the internet you should reference the information itself (name of author, date if available, title of article) and also say when you accessed the information and where from. For example:

> Davies, D. (1995) 'Recovered memory: uses and abuses', accessed 24 February 1998, available from *http://www.mon.ac.uk/staff/~davies/rmt.htm*.

Generally you shouldn't reference lecture notes. If you want to use something from a lecture, find it in a book or journal article and reference that. Ask the lecturer if you're not sure where to find the information.

Some references in your list will be primary references: references to a source you have read yourself. Others will be secondary references: references to something you've found when reading another source, like the Freud example from the Eysenck book mentioned above. When you put secondary references in your reference list, give the full reference itself and also the full reference for the book you got it from. For example:

> Freud, S. (1915) 'Repression', in Freud's *Collected Papers,* Vol. IV. London: Hogarth, cited in Eysenck, M. (2000) *Psychology: A Student's Handbook.* Hove: Psychology Press.

There is some variation across psychology departments about how to deal with secondary references, so check how yours prefers them to be referenced both in the text and in the reference list.

Preparing presentations

Psychology courses often have group presentations as part of the assessment. It's unlikely that you'll get through your whole psychology course without doing one of these. Students find them very scary, but they are excellent experience for later life because most jobs involve teamwork and you'll probably have to talk in front of a group at some stage, even if it's just at a wedding! However, if your fear about presentations goes beyond the usual nerves to the extreme symptoms of a phobia, talk it over with a student doctor or counsellor who should be able to exempt you.

For everyone else, below are seven helpful rules for planning presentations.

Rule 1: Put yourself in the shoes of the people who will be listening
Remember they haven't done all the reading in the area that you have, so explain things simply and clearly. Be aware that people can't take in a lot of information when listening to presentations. Stick to a few key points, using lots of examples to illustrate them and/or evidence to support them.

Rule 2: Check out your environment beforehand
Know what props you'll have, how big the room is and how many people will be there so you won't get any surprises. Ensure any equipment (like the overhead projector) is working. Arrange the chairs so that people sit where you want them. Open the windows if it's too warm. Have a bottle of water handy in case your throat goes dry. Wear comfortable clothes.

Rule 3: Prepare fully beforehand
Write out the aims of the talk and ensure that you meet these. Formulate an overall structure like with an essay. Have a beginning, a middle and an end. Keep the talk concise and ensure you can say everything you plan in the time you have. In a group presentation this may only be five minutes. Initially you'll feel this is a lot of time to fill. However, the most common mistake students make is having far too much to say. Practise your presentation through several times to make sure it fits the time you have. Rehearse it at least twice, preferably in front of friends who can give you feedback.

When working in a group, prepare and rehearse together or you might find yourselves saying the same things, or one person might eat into everyone else's time. Arrange at least three group meetings in the time between being told your presentation topic and doing the presentation.

Prepare answers to possible questions that people might ask after the talk. You'll probably be marked on this too. If possible, get a copy of the mark sheet your tutor will be using to ensure you meet all the criteria.

Rule 4: Have good props
The easiest thing to use is overhead transparencies (OHTs) with information either written on them or photocopied on from a computer printout (technical staff can help you to do this). OHTs give the audience something to focus on and help you to structure the talk. Don't have too many OHTs or too much written on each one. A good rule of thumb is about five OHTs for a fifteen minute talk. Information on OHTs should be in bullet points, not full sentences. Diagrams, graphs and pictures are good, but make them simple and clear. Font should be no smaller than 18 point. Ensure the writing on the OHTs is permanent; sweaty hands can easily smudge impermanent ink! The first person to talk should have an introductory OHT, overviewing the talk. The last person should have a concluding OHT drawing it all together.

You can use other props to make the presentation interesting for those watching. For example, some of my students used a clip from the film *Nightmare on Elm Street* to demonstrate a sleep recording device and role-played famous studies on sleep in front of the class. Test videos, tapes and computer equipment beforehand as these can go wrong. Handouts are helpful because they give the audience something to follow and take away.

Involving the audience keeps them interested. You can give them a short questionnaire to do, ask them to vote on the outcome of a study, or break them into small groups to come up with an answer to a question and then feed back to the rest of the group. Obviously you couldn't do this for your whole presentation because you also have to display your knowledge, but it's good to include a little audience participation, and this can put you more at ease too.

Rule 5: Make your delivery clear

Talk slowly. Generally we talk too fast when we present. Even if it sounds slow to you, it will probably be about the right speed for the audience. Pause a little at the end of each OHT to give them time to take in what you've said. Talk loudly enough, projecting to the back row of the room, so everyone can hear. Don't pace up and down or fidget. Use body language; point to the relevant information on the overhead projector. Vary your eye contact: look around the room focusing on different people at different times. If this is too scary, just look towards the back of the room.

Most importantly, don't read out your presentation: this is dull to listen to and hard to concentrate on. Write it in note form rather than word for word and you can talk around it rather than reading it out. Having your notes clearly written on numbered cards means you won't get lost or forget what you were going to say.

Rule 6: Use appropriate content

As I've said, it's vital to tailor content to the audience to make sure they understand what you're saying. Avoid jargon terms or mentioning things you don't completely understand. Think of four main messages you want people to take away from the talk and get these across clearly, repeating them and including them in the introduction and conclusion. It's OK to make the same point a few times because that helps it to sink in.

Generally the marker will look for the following things in terms of content, so use this as a checklist:

- Have you described the key points in this topic?
- Have you presented a well-balanced argument (presenting both sides of any debates covered)?
- Have you given some critical analysis of the issues (weighing up strengths and weakness of theories, studies, etc.)?
- Have you used information from a range of sources (providing a reference list on an OHT or handout)?

They'll also look for a clear presentation with easy-to-read visual aids and a good structure that flows well from one person to the next.

Rule 7: Beat the nerves!

Everyone has different ways of doing this. Remember that the people you are talking to are your peers; they all have to do the same thing themselves so they are likely to be sympathetic. Breathing exercises can help just before the presentation. Here is one:

- Close your eyes, breathe in deeply and exhale.
- Breathe in counting to four as you do so.

- Hold your breath for the count of four.
- Exhale while counting to eight.
- Repeat this several times.

The best way to beat the nerves is to be as well prepared as possible. Practise several times and ensure you have everything you need. Think of the sense of achievement getting through the presentation will give you. They really do get easier every time. I was terrified the first time I gave one and now I can lecture to two hundred people without breaking into a sweat! If you do make a mistake, don't worry: it happens to everyone sometimes and other people forget it much more quickly than you do.

Preparing for exams

The final common type of assessment on psychology courses is the exam. Some courses use multiple-choice exams, some short answer questions, some essay questions and some a combination. Here are some general tips for revision and for the exam itself.

Revision tips

- Get hold of past papers from tutors. List questions that have come up before in each area of the course. Ensure you could answer these for all the areas you are revising. This also gives you a feel for the types of questions that are set: whether they are straightforward or more complex, and whether they each relate to one topic or require you to synthesise your learning from across the different topics. The questions at the end of each chapter of this book and in the final chapter may also be helpful to practise on.

  Find out how many questions you need to answer out of how many topics from the module. For example, you may only have to answer five questions out of twelve that are set. Don't take risks, but it's often sensible to be selective in revision. If you can choose topics, pick ones that:

  - you understand and find interesting (these are easier to remember);
  - cover a large part of the course (e.g. revise two related topics, then you can answer questions on either, bringing in anything relevant from the other).

- For essay answer exams, think about how to structure answers in each area. What are the key things to mention? To practise, cut down essays to 500 words or less, only retaining the really important bits and the structure.
- Revise with other people. This is less boring and we learn well by teaching others. Test each other.
- Go to revision sessions provided by the department.
- Keep going over the information you have from your lecture notes and extra reading, summarising it down until you have a small core amount of information to revise. Diagrams and lists of key points are good.
- Figure out how long you will have for each answer before you go into the exam. Take everything you need with you (pen, back-up pen, ruler, watch, student card, drink, tissues).

--- CRUCIAL TIP ---

A good way of memorising little chunks of information is to repeat them to yourself before going to sleep. You generally wake up remembering them. Write key information, like the 'crucial concepts' from this book, on Post-it notes and stick them up to keep reminding you. The toilet door is a good place for such information!

Exam tips

- Read the exam format. If you have to answer one question from section A, one from section B and one from either, make sure you do this. If in doubt, ask the invigilator.

- Read the question. For essays or short answers, ensure you understand what the question is getting at before you plan your answer. If you don't quite understand but have to answer it, use your introduction to explain how you've interpreted the question and what you intend to discuss. Write something even if you're unsure. In my worst exam I didn't understand the questions. I spent an hour of the three hour exam writing things and crossing them out because I was so uncertain. I nearly ran out in tears. Finally I just explained what I thought the questions were asking for and answered that. I got a B!

- For essay or short answer exams, spend 5–10 minutes at the beginning planning your answers in the front of the answer book (including any really important information you might forget). You'll feel calmer after this.

- Watch the clock. Give the same amount of time to each answer. People often spend far too long on the first few questions. They then get low marks for the later ones and really pull their grade down.

- A good, short essay is better than a long one that's poorly structured or not related to the question.

- Subheadings and diagrams make essays easier to read. Examiners like this!

- For essay exams, follow the advice given for writing coursework essays above. You don't need to reference thoroughly in exams, but mention key theorists/researchers and roughly when they were working. For example, you could say 'in the early twentieth century, Freud proposed his theory of defence mechanisms'.

- If you're running out of time, finish your answer in note form, you can still get marks for this.

- Don't panic! If exams really scare you, get support and try the breathing exercise given above.

CRUCIAL TIP

Always answer each question even if you're not sure about it. In multiple choice exams, even if you don't know the answer you may get it right by chance. In short answer exams students often bring their marks down by leaving questions out. If you write something you'll get at least some marks. If you write nothing you'll get nothing. Compare the overall scores for the following two students who had to answer five questions. Both were sure about the first two questions, less sure about the third one and really unsure about the last two. Student 1 had a go at the last two questions, bringing in some other things she knew even though she wasn't sure they were relevant. Student 2 left them blank and spent the extra time writing really thorough answers to the first two questions.

Student 1: 65 60 45 35 25 Overall grade = 46
Student 2: 70 65 45 0   0   Overall grade = 36

So student 1 passed whereas student 2 failed, with a ten-point difference between their grades. A very similar thing happens if you spend most of your time on the first few questions, so give the same amount of time to each question.

The rest of this book gives advice on writing answers on specific topics in psychology. Good luck in all your assessments and enjoy the rest of the book!

Section 4

Further reading

The following books give extra advice about study skills in psychology:

Collins, S. C. and Kneale, P. E. (2001) *Study Skills For Psychology Students: A Practical Guide*. London: Arnold.

Eysenck, M. (2000) *Psychology: A Student's Handbook*. Hove: Psychology Press.

Heffernan, T. M. (1997) *A Student's Guide to Studying Psychology*. Hove: Psychology Press.

These books give good advice about English, grammar and punctuation:

Kirkman, J. (1993) *Full Marks: Advice on Punctuation for Scientific and Technical Writing*. Malborough: Ramsbury Books.

Russell, S. (1993) *Grammar, Structure and Style*. Oxford: Oxford University Press.

Chapter 1
Psychology and its history

Chapter summary

In order to understand psychology as it is today, we need to know something about its past. History can help us appreciate how psychology came to be the way it is and where current theories and approaches came from. This chapter traces key ideas in psychology, placing them in their historical context.

Assessment targets

Target 1: Describing what psychology is
People are often confused about what psychology is and what psychologists do. This chapter will help you to differentiate psychology from the other things that it is often confused with. It will also introduce you to common definitions of psychology and explain what psychology looks like as a discipline today. Question 1 at the end of the chapter tests your grasp of these points.

Target 2: Explaining the origins of psychology
It has been said that psychology has a short history but a long past. As a discipline it has been around for just over a century, but it has much older roots in philosophy and biology. This chapter will help you to understand these early origins, and the ways in which psychology drew on them. Question 2 at the end of the chapter tests your ability to describe these origins.

Target 3: Understanding the history of psychology as a discipline
After psychology became a discipline in its own right several different schools of psychology emerged. This chapter helps you to understand these, the approaches they took and how they fit into the history of the discipline. Question 3 at the end of the chapter tests your understanding of the history of psychology.

How will you be assessed on this?

Section 1 of this chapter introduces what psychology is. It is rather important to know this is in order to carry out any assessment on a psychology course! However, many students get confused between psychology and related disciplines in their essays. This section should help you to be very clear about this, and about why we need to study the history of psychology. Section 2 outlines this history, helping you to understand the origins of the theories and debates that we cover later in the book, which you will be assessed on. You may also be asked essay and exam questions on introductory modules about the origins of psychology or the differences between the early schools. Section 3 provides you with basic knowledge about psychology today that you need to have for any assessment, and in order to understand your reading and lectures.

Section 1

What is psychology?

In this section we will cover definitions of psychology and why we need to understand its history.

What is psychology?

Popular perceptions of psychology are often pretty confused. You will probably have encountered this already when you've told people that you're doing a psychology course. It's likely that some people will have responded by saying either 'I'd better be careful what I say' or 'go on, analyse me then'. People like me, who have been doing psychology for several years, get pretty bored with these jokes! The perception is that psychologists can uncover people's secrets. Perhaps sadly, most of us do not have any such magical talents. Psychologists **do** study how people think and behave. However, most of us do not attempt to analyse individual people in depth. Usually, we are involved in studying one small area of thought or behaviour such as how people remember faces, what areas of the brain perceive colour, how children learn language or how people form attitudes about things.

--- CRUCIAL TIP ---

To get a good idea of what people in general know about psychology, ask some friends to tell you what they think psychology is and what psychologists do, and to name any psychologists they've heard of. Then compare their responses to the information in this section.

We will see where some of these misconceptions about psychology come from shortly. First of all, lets look at the word.

'Psychology' derives from two Greek words: psyche and logos. Psyche (pronounced 'sigh-key') is from the Greek word for mind or soul. Psyche was a Greek goddess who fell in love with Eros (the Greek version of Cupid, the god of love). Their story was the original basis of the fairy tale 'Beauty and the Beast'. The Greek letter Ψ (psi) is now used as the international symbol for psychology. Logos means 'knowledge'. All 'ologies' contain this word, and it means the 'study of' something.

Putting the two bits of the word together would give us the definition 'the study of the mind', which seems pretty straightforward. However, most psychologists would not accept this as a definition of psychology today. There are three main problems with it.

- Most psychologists today would not use the word 'mind', since it implies something separate to the physical body and brain. They would prefer the term 'mental processes', since these can be seen as happening within the brain. So perhaps we should change the definition to 'the study of mental processes'.

- Contemporary psychology is not just concerned with inner mental processes; it is also concerned with outward behaviour. So maybe we need to change the definition to 'the study of mental processes and behaviour'.

- Some psychologists, particularly behaviourists, have argued that psychology shouldn't study mental processes at all because they can't be examined directly. So perhaps we need to change the definition to 'the study of behaviour'. But this doesn't quite work because many psychologists, particularly cognitivists, do believe that we can study mental processes and experiences. They are not just interested in the behaviour itself, but in understanding **why** it happens the way it does. They do look at outward behaviour, but mainly to make inferences about internal processes such as how memory works.

There is an additional problem, which is that most psychologists would want to go further than the word 'study', since this doesn't cover the rigorous techniques that they use. They would prefer to use the word 'science', although it is not always clear what this means, and some would argue that psychology is not a science (see Chapter 4).

Most psychologists today accept the working definition of psychology as 'the scientific study of the behaviour of individuals and their mental processes' (Zimbardo, 1992). However, it is worth remembering that there are debates over both the content of study (mental process, behaviour or both), and how it is done (whether it is scientific). Note that Zimbardo uses 'individuals' instead of 'humans'; this is because some psychologists study animals, either because they are interested in them in their own right, or so that they can draw inferences from animals to humans.

CRUCIAL TIP

Students often start their essays with dictionary definitions of the terms used in the essay question, for example 'psychology'. This is rarely appropriate because dictionaries do not give psychological definitions. It is important to be clear what the terms mean, but it is better to find the definitions devised by prominent psychologists (from a textbook or a dictionary of psychology, e.g. Stratton and Hayes, 1999), and don't spend too long going through the definitions of every single term.

What psychology is not

If we return to the popular misconceptions of psychology, most of these seem to come about because people confuse psychology with three other 'psych' words: psychotherapy, psychiatry and psychoanalysis.

Psychotherapy is pretty much the same as counselling. Psychotherapists and counsellors are people who use therapies to help their clients with psychological and emotional problems, such as depression or panic attacks, often in one-to-one sessions. They generally do not have qualifications in psychology, but have taken training courses to learn how to use the various therapies, many of which originated in psychological theories.

Some kinds of applied psychologists do specialise in helping people with therapy. These clinical and counselling psychologists are similar to psychotherapists although they do have a background in psychology. However, there is a lot more to psychology than these branches (see Chapter 3).

Psychiatrists are also concerned with psychological disorders. However, their background is in medicine rather than psychology. Psychiatrists are trained medical doctors who have then specialised in psychiatry. They may use similar therapies to psychotherapists and clinical psychologists, but they are also qualified to prescribe drugs (which the other two groups are not). The character 'Frasier' on the popular TV show is a psychiatrist, as is Dr Raj Persaud who often appears on morning television. People often think they are psychologists.

There are two main differences between psychology and psychotherapy/psychiatry:

- Most psychologists look at 'normal' behaviour, rather than what happens when psychological functioning goes wrong.
- Most psychologists do not work one-to-one with clients but study a number of people.

If you ask some friends to name a psychologist, as suggested earlier, you'll probably find that most of them say 'Freud'. Freud was actually a medical doctor, who founded a school of psychology known as the psychoanalytic school.

CRUCIAL CONCEPT

Psychoanalysis (or **psychoanalytic theory**) is a range of theories about the development of human personality and emotions, and an associated method of therapy, based on the writings of the Austrian doctor, Sigmund Freud (1856–1939). The key idea was that people could be cured of psychological dysfunctions by bringing unconscious material into the conscious mind. Freud also saw adult behaviour as being strongly influenced by childhood experiences.

People often assume that Freud's psychoanalytic theories form the basis of modern psychology, and that modern psychologists, like Freud, try to analyse people to uncover their hidden desires. Really, very few modern psychologists belong to the psychoanalytic school, and most are very sceptical of psychoanalytic theories. However, psychoanalysis is still popular on some psychotherapy courses, and also among some academics in disciplines like English and cultural studies (see Chapter 2).

Psychology is occasionally confused with 'parapsychology', a small branch of research devoted to investigating so-called paranormal phenomena like mind-reading (telepathy) and predicting the future (precognition). Most psychologists are sceptical about para-psychology because there are frequently non-paranormal explanations for seemingly supernatural experiences. For example, Hyman (1977) shows that, although psychics may seem amazingly accurate, they actually use 'cold reading': picking up on obvious things about a person, giving them a 'stock spiel' that would apply to anyone, listening to them and telling them what they want to hear. Shermer (1997) shows that many things we take to be paranormal can be explained by our lack of understanding of statistics and coincidence. We think it's spooky when we decide to phone someone and they ring at the very moment we were about to dial their number. Actually, it would be much more unusual if that never happened. Also, we forget all the times when that person did not phone just as we were about to call them. We tend to remember hits and ignore misses, which is why people think it's amazing when a psychic gets something right about them, even when they have said a few wrong things too. Parapsychology is a marginalised field because there is so much scepticism in psychology about the existence of the paranormal.

Two other minor fields of psychological research which people often think are much bigger, or perhaps even the whole of psychology, are criminal psychology, because of popular TV programmes and films like *Silence of the Lambs*, and psychometrics, because people often think of intelligence and personality tests when they think of psychology, and these are what psychometrics focuses on.

The confusion between psychology and parapsychology may explain why some people think that psychologists can read their minds. This may also be reinforced by the unrealistic depiction of criminal psychologists like 'Cracker' or Robson Green's character in 'Wire in the Blood' who have special knowledge enabling them to catch criminals even when experienced police officers are stumped. Quizzes in magazines and popular self-help books often claim to reveal hidden things about our personalities. People may assume that these come from 'real' psychology or psychometrics when in fact they generally do not. See Chapter 3 for more about criminal psychology and psychometric testing.

Finally, psychology also differs from the related discipline of sociology. Sociology investigates behaviour too. However, it studies the social behaviour of large groups of people in societies or subcultures, whereas psychology examines particular aspects of the mental processes and behaviour of individuals or small groups of people, with only the area of social psychology focusing on social behaviour (see Chapter 3). Sociologists and psychologists generally have different levels of explanation (see reductionism in Chapter 5), and sociologists use more qualitative methods (see Chapter 4).

Understanding the history of psychology

Now that we understand what psychology is, we can move on to examining its history. You might ask yourself why it is important to understand the history of psychology, especially when some of the theories and methods of the past are no longer used.

You should already have one answer to this question: there is a lot of misunderstanding and disagreement about what psychology is, and history can help to explain where this comes from. For example, it tells us more about the debate over whether psychology should be the study of the mind or behaviour, and where psychoanalysis fits in.

Jones and Elcock (2001) put forward four reasons for studying the history of psychology:

- It helps us understand psychology today – the background to current theories and debates (see above).

- Interest – the history of psychology is a very interesting area of study in its own right.

- Learning lessons from the past – if we are replacing previously accepted theories or methods with new ones, we need to know what was wrong with the old ones so that we can avoid these problems. We might come up with a new theory which is very similar to an old one (as happens quite often in psychology). We need to recognise the old theory in our new one and know what the weaknesses of it were. Also, we can improve on methods used in the past that were invalid or ethically questionable (see Chapter 3), and recognise any biases in past theories which are to be avoided (see Chapter 4).

- Understanding the relationship between psychology and its social and historical context – histories of psychology often leave out the relationship between psychology and the society it operates in. By including this we can understand how theories are influenced by the social context and political situation of the time and place psychologists live in (see Chapter 5). We can also see the impact of psychological theories upon society.

Many histories of psychology also tend to be 'present-centred'. In other words, they tell the story of the discipline as a progressive process of finding the truth, as if the development of psychology inevitably led to the current state of affairs which is the 'right' way of seeing things. The accepted positions in psychology today may seem just as flawed to people in the future as those in the past do to us now. Keep this in mind when you are reading about the history of psychology and psychology today.

Section summary

In this section we have seen that there is no universally accepted definition of psychology, and have explored some possible definitions and the problems with them. We have also differentiated psychology from psychotherapy, psychiatry, psychoanalysis and some other areas it is often confused with. Finally, we have explored why it is useful to understand the history of psychology, which will set us up for section 2 on this topic.

Quick test

What is an accepted definition of psychology? Explain how psychology differs from the other activities that it is often confused with.

Section 2

The history of psychology

This section outlines the roots of psychology (in philosophy and biology), and describes the chronological development of psychology as a discipline, covering the various schools that emerged.

The origins of psychology

Figure 1.1 displays many of the significant events in psychological thinking when it was part of philosophy and since it has been a discipline in its own right. These will be expanded on in this section, and you should refer back to the time line to remind yourself when the various events occurred.

ANCIENT TIMES
(800 BC – 400AD)

~585 BC – Thales of Miletus proposes a crucial role for the brain in mental experience.

~400 BC – Hippocrates proposes a relationship between personality characteristics and body type.

~350 BC – Aristotle wrote the first textbook of psychology *De Anima* (concerning the soul), questioning the relationship between the soul and the body. The soul is seen as giving life to the body.

MIDDLE AGES
(400 – 1500)

During this period, intellectual life in Europe is dominated by Christian theology; objective investigation of behaviour and mental experience are discouraged. People seen as having souls and subject to the will of God.

EARLY MODERN PERIOD
(1500-1800)

1650 – René Descartes distinguishes between mind (mental experiences – thoughts, feelings and sensations) and body (physical processes), proposing these interact in the pineal gland in the brain and influence each other.

1651 – Thomas Hobbes claims that mental experiences are just a product of motion of physical matter.

1690 – John Locke extends Hobbes' views claiming that a newborn mind is a *tabula rasa* (blank slate), formally beginning British empiricism and *associationism* (later elaborated by Mills in the nineteenth century).

1748 – La Mettrie writes *L'Homme machine* (The Human Machine). Part of French materialism, proposing that mental experiences are just 'epiphenomena' – trivial by-products of brain processes – and unimportant.

Late 1700s – Franz Joseph Gall invents phrenology – location of mental faculties in specific regions of the brain – highly developed faculties associated with bumps on the skull.

MODERN PERIOD
(1800-now)

1850 – Gustav Fechner develops experimental and statistical procedures to measure relationships between physical stimuli and sensations.

1859 – Charles Darwin publishes *The Origin of Species* – the theory of evolution through natural selection.

1861 – Paul Broca provides first link between psychological function (speech) and specific area of brain (Broca's).

1874 – Karl Wernicke discovers brain area associated with language comprehension (Wernicke's).

1879 – Wilhelm Wundt founds first experimental psychology laboratory in Leipzig, Germany (*structuralism*).

1890 – William James publishes the influential *Principles of Psychology* in the USA.

1896 – Edward Thorndike reports his findings on animal learning (*functionalism*).

1900 – Sigmund Freud publishes *The Interpretation of Dreams*, setting out many aspects of *psychoanalysis*.

1906 – Ivan Pavlov publishes the findings of his studies on classical conditioning.

1912 – Max Wertheimer publishes the earliest account of *Gestalt psychology*.

1913 – J B Watson breaks away from functionalism with an article that launches *behaviourism*.

1938 – B F Skinner publishes his work on operant conditioning in *The Behaviour of Organisms*.

1951 – Carl Rogers publishes *Client Centred Therapy* – precursor to forming Association of Humanistic Psychology (1962) – *humanism*.

1956 – 'Cognitive revolution' – at a Massachusetts Institute of Technology (MIT) conference, Chomsky presents a paper on his theory of language, Miller on short-term memory and Newell and Simon on problem solving. Bruner et al. investigate concept formation from a cognitive perspective. They discuss the possibility of computers that could 'behave' or 'think' intelligently (artificial intelligence) – *cognitivism*.

1972 – a 'new paradigm'? Harré and Secord publish *The Explanation of Social Behaviour*, drawing together criticisms of scientific psychology and proposing an alternative (see end of Chapter 4).

THE STUDY OF PSYCHOLOGICAL MATTERS IS PART OF PHILOSOPHY

PSYCHOLOGY IS A DISCIPLINE IN ITS OWN RIGHT

Ψ

Figure 1.1 Time-line of psychology and its origins

From the time line you can see what Ebbinghaus, the early German psychologist, meant when he said that psychology had a long past but a short history. Most modern psychologists agree that psychology became a discipline in its own right in 1879, although this is a fairly arbitrary date. The choice of 1879 says a lot about how we view psychology today, because it can be seen as marking the beginning of psychology as a science (with Wundt's laboratory), and modern psychologists place a great deal of importance on the scientific nature of the discipline (see Chapter 4).

However, philosophers were considering psychological matters for hundreds of years prior to this. Many philosophical ideas had an important impact on early psychology, as did several theories from biology, a science with a slightly longer history than psychology (see Figure 1.2).

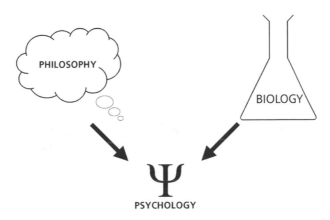

Figure 1.2 Two main roots of psychology

Roots in philosophy

As you can see from the time-line, the first people we know to have systematically theorised about psychological issues were the ancient Greek philosophers. Some of the answers they came up with may seem strange to us today, but make sense in the context of what they knew and believed at the time. The important thing is that they thought to ask some vital questions, which continued to tax philosophers for hundreds of years.

The ancient Greek philosophers were the first to realise that the brain had a vital role in mental experiences, although there was some debate about this. Plato thought that only reason resided in the brain, with desire being in the liver and courage in the heart. Aristotle located all mental experiences in the heart.

The Greek thinkers were also the first to propose theories of personality (or temperament, as they called it). Hippocrates' classification of people into four groups was widely accepted throughout the Middle Ages. People were either sanguine (optimistic), melancholic (depressive), choleric (short-tempered) or phlegmatic (apathetic), based on the balance of four fluids (or humours) in their body.

Perhaps the most important contribution of the ancient Greek philosophers was their consideration of the association between the mind (or soul) and the body. Aristotle was the first to argue for an intimate relationship between the two, suggesting a close link between biology and psychology that is in line with many contemporary theories.

There was little investigation into psychological matters during the Middle Ages, and the next philosopher to have a major impact on the development of psychological thinking was Descartes (pronounced 'Day-cart') in the 1600s. He continued the mind–body debate, arguing that only humans possessed a mind (or soul) and that it was separate from the body, without a physical reality. Descartes' theory was problematic because it couldn't explain how mental experience could affect physical processes and vice versa. For example, being sad (mental) makes us cry (physical), being hit (physical) makes us feel pain (mental). This is the mind–body problem that philosophers have grappled with ever since. Descartes' answer was that the mind and the body influence each other via the pineal gland in the brain.

In contrast to Descartes, two other writers in the 1600s, Hobbes and Locke, argued that only physical matter existed, and that mental processes were a result of 'matter in motion', the nerves and the brain. They were empiricists, who tried to use systematic, objective methods of study rather than just intuition or reasoning. This can be contrasted with Descartes' ideas, which suggest that mental experiences cannot be studied scientifically since they have no physical reality.

CRUCIAL CONCEPT

Empiricism is the philosophical school of thought which argues that only things that can be directly observed or measured can be meaningfully studied. This was very influential on psychology, and is the root of the term 'empirical' (see Chapter 4).

Hobbes and Locke also believed that the mind develops as it interacts with the environment, through sensory experiences, whereas Descartes believed that ideas were innate. This was an early version of the nature–nurture debate (see Chapter 5).

The 1700s are sometimes called 'the Age of Reason' because it was during this time that the rational approach to the world of ideas became popular. Newton's theory of gravity was immensely successful, and created the impression that natural science would be able to explain everything before long. This had a rather negative impact on the development of psychology. Purely physical solutions to the mind–body problem became fashionable, especially among the French materialist philosophers like La Mettrie. He proposed that mental experiences are real, but are only the trivial by-products (or 'epiphenomena') of physical brain processes. This epiphenomenology had a damaging effect because philosophers began to regard mental experiences such as thoughts and feelings as not worth investigating since they couldn't have any effects.

Psychology was only able to grow into an independent discipline once this way of thinking had gone into decline, at the beginning of the 1800s. At this time the mind–body problem re-emerged as epiphenomenology was undermined by the collapse of phrenology (see Figure 1.1), the discovery that hypnosis was a purely psychological process (not an epiphenomena of any physical substance) and the finding that several mental disorders could not be explained by physical disorders. For example, many patients with hysteria suffered paralysis, loss of sensation or even blindness with no apparent biological cause.

One final philosophical idea that influenced early psychology was another contribution of Aristotle, the ancient Greek philosopher, which was also put forward by Locke in the 1600s. This philosophy is known as associationism, and was elaborated in the 1800s by John Stuart Mill and others. Associationism is reflected in the theories of many of the early experimental psychologists and psychoanalysts (for example the Gestalt psychologists and Freud).

CRUCIAL CONCEPT

Associationism is the philosophy that ideas have a tendency to become associated with one another. Complex ideas are built up from simpler ones. John Stuart Mill and his father proposed several laws of mental association, notably: **contiguity** (ideas become associated when they are close in time or space, for example we associate the colour green and grass because we often see the two together), **similarity** (similar ideas tend to become associated, for example oranges and lemons) and **frequency** (the more frequently ideas occur together, the more strongly they are associated).

Roots in biology

The other area that had a major influence on psychology was biological research. This thrived under French materialism since people were looking for scientific explanations for the function of living things to replace the miraculous or magical explanations held before 'the Age of Reason'. Physiology became an established branch of science in the late 1700s and led to many studies of bodily processes. For example, Galvani found that a frog's leg moves when an electrical current is passed through it, suggesting that the nervous system functions through electrical impulses. This was vital in furthering understanding of the physiology of the nervous system.

A group of German thinkers and physiologists began to study mental activity in the early 1800s: Helmholtz proposed different nerves for the different senses and the three types of colour receptor in the eye. Ernst Weber and Fechner investigated the relationship between physical intensity and perceived intensity of stimuli like weight, sound and light, e.g. how much heavier we estimate weight to be when it is doubled. These ideas strongly influenced the branch of cognitive psychology that focuses on perception, still known as psycho-physics, although back then Weber recognised it as a branch of physiology, and Fechner as a branch of philosophy.

Another idea that had an enormous impact on early psychology was evolution. Evolutionary theories were circulating in the early 1800s but gained huge impetus when Charles Darwin's book, *The Origin of Species*, was published in 1859.

CRUCIAL CONCEPT

Darwin's **theory of evolution** had three fundamental ideas: variation, heredity and selection. There is variation among individual members of a species, but offspring resemble their parents (having inherited their characteristics). Those individuals best adapted to the environment produce more offspring than others, so their characteristics are most likely to continue. This is the process of 'natural selection', explaining how new species gradually evolve.

Darwin's theories had several important implications for early psychology:

- Since all species are biologically related to each other through evolution and humans differ from other animals in complexity only, a lot can be learned about humans by studying other animals. Animals are simpler systems and therefore easier to understand. Findings can then be generalised to humans.

- It encouraged the study of inherited traits. Evolutionary psychologists have seen aspects of human behaviour as being inherited (see Chapter 5).

- The idea that members of a species vary in how well equipped they are for their environment led to the study of individual differences. For example, Galton, Darwin's cousin, studied individual differences in intelligence, which led to a huge area of research in psychology (e.g. Spearman, Burt and Eysenck).

One final area of research which influenced early psychology was the work of Broca and Wernicke. Through studying patients with brain damage, they discovered links between psychological functions and specific regions of the brain. The field of neuropsychology continues to study such associations today.

The emergence of psychology

So we can see that the many factors came together for psychology to emerge as a discipline in its own right, particularly the popularity of empirical scientific research, the rediscovery of mental philosophy (after epiphenomenology), and the development of biology. The lack of distinct boundaries between the various disciplines which combined to produce psychology can be seen in Wundt (pronounced 'Voont'). He was a physiologist by training who had worked with Helmholtz, but became professor of 'scientific philosophy' at Leipzig University prior to setting up the first psychology laboratory.

The word 'psychology' had been around since 1693, when a physical dictionary defined two parts of 'the description of man': 'anatomy, which treats of the Body, and psychology, which treats of the Soul' (Colman, 1999, p. 161). However, the word only began to be widely used and understood in the 1830s, and it was only after 1879 that a deliberate attempt was made to separate psychology from philosophy, to organise professional psychologists into their own community and to teach scientific psychology in universities. Wundt was the first to use the term 'experimental psychology', and to call it 'a new domain of science'.

The development of psychology

As psychology developed as a discipline, a number of different schools of thought emerged (see Figure 1.3). A 'school' consisted of a group of psychologists who shared common beliefs about subject matter (what aspects should be studied) and method (how they should study them). Most schools developed out of the rejection of the ideas of earlier schools, as we will see. However, each school did not replace the last; rather they often existed alongside each other. We don't really have schools of psychology any more, although the schools did influence the contemporary approaches to psychology that we cover in Chapter 2.

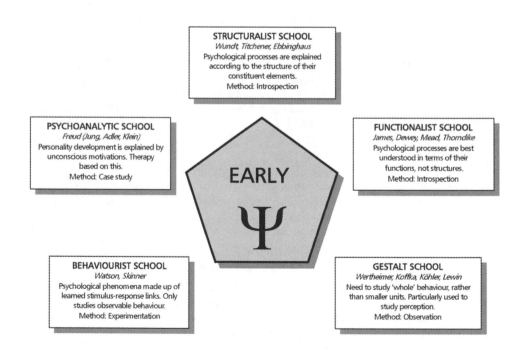

Figure 1.3 The early schools of psychology

CRUCIAL TIP

If you are taking other subjects alongside your psychology course, such as sociology, media studies, English or philosophy, you might come across some of these words there as well. For example, **structuralism** was not just a psychological school, it is also the name applied to the branch of linguistics that understands language in terms of the signs that make it up. There are structuralist, functionalist and psychoanalytic approaches to other disciplines besides psychology. Try not to get confused by this. Here you just need to know what these ideas meant in psychology.

Now we will look at the ideas of each of these different schools, along with some of the key people within each school.

Structuralism

Wundt and his many collaborators in Germany in the 1880s founded the structuralist school of psychology. The structuralist psychologists tried to break mental experiences down into their constituent parts to see what the basic elements were and how they combined. The idea was that these elements were something like the chemical elements (hydrogen, oxygen, nitrogen, etc.) that combine in certain structures to give water or air. The elements the structuralists were interested in were sensations (sights, sounds, tastes, smells, etc.), feelings (love, anger, fear, etc.) and ideas (images of the imagination or memory). According to this way of thinking, an experience like going to the pub would be composed of many independent sensations, feelings and images, which would be combined into a certain structure by the mind.

The method used to investigate these elements was known as introspection. This means the examination of one's own mental state. People were trained to follow rigorous rules to consider their own mental processes and to report upon them. For example, introspecting about a tree would involve describing sensations experienced in terms of its shape, colour, size, texture, etc.

CRUCIAL CONCEPT

Structuralism explains psychological phenomena by understanding how their basic elements are structured. Examples include explaining aggression from the structure of the brain or proposing a hypothetical structure for personality.

Structuralism was taken up by Titchener, who studied with Wundt prior to becoming a professor of psychology in the US, where he developed and adapted the ideas. Structuralism declined in the 1930s, partly due to the advent of Nazism in Germany and Titchener's death in the US.

The schools of functionalism, behaviourism and Gestalt psychology all developed, to some degree, as reactions against structuralist psychology. However, we can still see the influence of structuralism in modern research on sensation perception, especially in the field of psychophysics.

Functionalism

One of the first US psychologists was William James, and he was a leading figure in functional psychology, along with John Dewey, a US philosopher and psychologist. The functionalists disagreed with the structuralists. They felt that psychological processes were best understood in terms of their function rather than their structure. They drew on evolutionary theory, proposing that consciousness enables humans to behave in ways that improve their chances of survival through adaptation to the environment. They argued that consciousness is needed for complex situations in which automatic, reflex ways of responding are not appropriate. However, once the adaptive conscious behaviours are repeated several times, they become habits, and conscious control disappears. For example, when learning a new skill like riding a bike or driving a car, at first we are conscious of every action, but soon it becomes automatic and we don't need to think consciously about each movement.

CRUCIAL CONCEPT

Functionalism introduced evolutionary ideas into psychology, explaining thoughts and behaviour in terms of their function for adapting the individual animal or human to its environment.

Functionalists such as James and Dewey were also very interested in applying psychology to practical problems such as education (see Chapter 3). Functionalists pioneered the use of animals in psychological research because of their evolutionary perspective. For example, Thorndike studied problem-solving in cats and dogs using special puzzle boxes which they could escape from by learning to pull a loop. Functionalism was gradually taken over by behaviourism in the 1920s and 1930s, which criticised its focus on mental processes and the methods it used. However, functionalism can be seen as an important bridge between structuralism and behaviourism (which retained some of functionalism's principles). We can still see the influence of functionalism in sociobiological theories of psychology today (those proposing an evolutionary basis of behaviour – see Chapter 5). Thorndike's finding that animals gradually learned how to escape from his boxes was built on by the behaviourist Skinner (see Chapter 2).

You can see from these two early schools of psychology that the discipline developed quickly in Germany and the US. You might expect that it would also develop in France and Britain, since these two countries were the home of most of the philosophers and biologists who pioneered the study of psychological matters. However, this was not the case. After epiphenomenology, the materialist, anti-psychological bias remained in France, and the influence of Descartes there meant that there was a resistance to empirical methods in relation to mental processes. In Britain, the academic world was very conservative and tended not to encourage new trends. The traditional universities also had strong links with the church. In 1877, Cambridge University turned down the opportunity to establish a psychological laboratory on the grounds that it would 'insult religion by putting the human soul in a pair of scales' (Colman, 1999, p. 163). Oxford University didn't officially teach experimental psychology until 1936.

Behaviourism

In 1913, the US psychologist, J. B. Watson broke away from functionalism and established the behaviourist school of psychology when he published a paper called 'Psychology as a behaviourist views it', arguing that psychology should only study observable behaviour that everyone could agree on. Until then, many functionalists had continued using the introspective techniques of the structuralists. For example, James used these to study what he called 'streams of consciousness' (the continuous flow of thoughts). Watson said that these techniques were unreliable and could not be checked for accuracy because they were reports of private experience. He argued that psychology should stop investigating such areas, and should never use the terms 'consciousness', 'mental states' or 'mind', since these were just by-products of physiological processes. You can see that this is a return to the epiphenomenology that predated psychology as a discipline.

CRUCIAL CONCEPT

Behaviourism is the school of psychology that focuses on observable behaviour and ignores mental processes. Behaviourists consider that all human behaviour consists of connections between a stimulus and a response. These are learnt through the process of 'conditioning'.

We will explore the ideas within behaviourism in more detail in Chapter 2, when we consider it as one of the main approaches to psychology. For now, it is just important for you to see how it represented a very different approach to functionalism and structuralism. Watson declared that the goal of psychology should be the prediction and control of behaviour, whereas the structuralist version of psychology did not involve prediction, control **or** behaviour. Behaviourism rejected the methods of functionalism, but retained the biological foundations, particularly the idea that animals and humans were not fundamentally different, so human behaviour could be learnt about by studying animal behaviour. B. F. Skinner's work from the late 1930s onwards particularly extended Watson's earlier principles and kept behaviourism going.

Behaviourism was criticised for being reductionist (see Chapter 5). Most modern psychologists do not agree that conditioned learning can explain all psychological phenomena, and today most tend to see some role for the study of mental processes. However, Watson's and Skinner's theories do form the basis of our current understanding of learning and are very important in many branches of applied psychology (see Chapter 3). Also, the emphasis on objective, scientific methods has shaped modern psychology (see Chapter 4). Some see Watson's paper as marking the first of two 'revolutions' in psychology: the 'behaviourist revolution'.

Gestalt psychology

Functionalism and behaviourism both emerged in the USA. Around the same time, Gestalt psychology emerged in Austria and Germany as a protest against both German structuralism and US behaviourism. The Gestalt psychologists opposed the idea, held by both structuralists and behaviourists, that the best way to understand a phenomenon was to break it down into its constituent parts.

CRUCIAL CONCEPT

Gestalt psychology particularly focused on perception, and proposed several principles of perceptual organisation, the most famous of which is 'the whole is greater than the sum of its parts'. This means that people perceive the world as a whole, not in terms of the individual elements that make it up. They believed that the brain had an innate ability to organise the things we perceive into meaningful patterns rather than perceiving separate elements.

A good example of this is the visual illusion involved in watching a movie. Movies are made up of still images run together fast, but what we see is 'greater than the sum of these parts' because we see a moving image. Wertheimer examined effects like this by using two lights a small distance apart. When there was a certain time interval between switching these lights on and off, people would report seeing one moving light rather than two distinct ones. Wertheimer called this effect the 'phi phenomenon'. The same type of thing occurs when we listen to a series of musical notes, but hear a tune. For example, the tunes 'Frère Jacques' and 'Three Blind Mice' are made up of the same notes (or elements), they are just ordered in a slightly different way. (Some further Gestalt principles of perceptual organisation are illustrated in Figure 1.4.)

Remembering back to the philosophy of associationism, you can see how Gestalt psychology was rooted in this, since associationists like John Stuart Mill also proposed that complex ideas are more than just the combination of the simple ideas that make them up. The Gestalt psychologists went further, arguing that to understand the mind, we must study overall patterns, configurations or 'wholes'. They argued that the brain always attempts to perceive things in the most meaningful way possible, although critics have pointed out that they never actually showed that the brain worked in this way or explained why.

Some Gestalt psychologists studied areas other than perception. For example, Köhler researched problem-solving. In one study he placed some food just out of reach of an ape, outside his cage. He gave the ape several sticks which, if slotted together, could reach the food. The ape did nothing for a while, and then suddenly solved the problem. Köhler argued that this was because all the elements for the solution were there, so the animal perceived the problem as a whole, formed a hypothesis about the solution and then put it into practice. This is known as 'insight learning'.

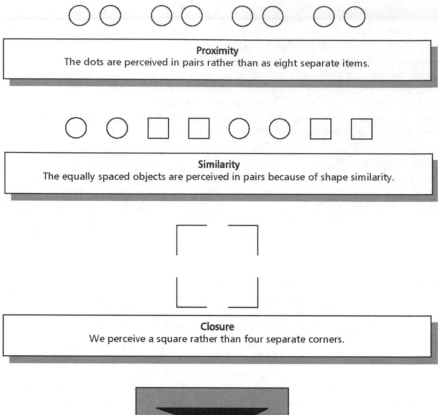

Proximity
The dots are perceived in pairs rather than as eight separate items.

Similarity
The equally spaced objects are perceived in pairs because of shape similarity.

Closure
We perceive a square rather than four separate corners.

Figure-ground
Focusing attention on an object (figure) causes it to stand out from the context (ground).
In an ambiguous figure like 'Rubin's vase', the figure and ground switch as the brain
switches attention from one to the other and back again.

Figure 1.4 Gestalt principles of perceptual organisation

Sadly, the influence of Gestalt psychology was diminished by the rise of Nazism in
Germany. In the 1920s and 1930s Wertheimer, Köhler and the others emigrated to the US,
where behaviourism had already taken hold. However, the Gestalt emphasis on 'cognitive'
aspects of psychology provided an important background to the 'cognitive revolution' in
1956, keeping some of these ideas alive during the dominance of behaviourism. Some
Gestalt ideas flourish today in the cognitive field of perception, and there is also a type of
Gestalt psychotherapy which draws on the ideas of the Gestalt psychologists to treat the
'whole' person.

Psychoanalysis

The final early school of psychology developed out of Freud's psychoanalysis, which we defined in section 1. The psychodynamic approach (which grew from the psychoanalytic school) is explained in greater detail in the next chapter. Here we just need to know that, unlike the other schools, this school was not made up of academic psychologists. All the other schools shared a common goal of understanding psychological processes. Freud, however, was a medical doctor, and his goal was to treat the neurotic patients who came to him. Therefore, his methods were very different from those devised by academic psychologists, and his theories were meant to be useful rather than experimentally testable. His followers, such as Jung, Adler and Klein, were also therapists rather than researchers.

The different social origin of psychoanalysis explains why it has never really been accepted by mainstream academic psychologists. However, we will see in the next chapter that the theories of Freud and his followers have had a huge impact on western culture in general, and many of his ideas have filtered into the areas of clinical and counselling psychology.

CRUCIAL TIP

Depending on the views of your lecturers, you may find that Freud is hardly mentioned in your degree course, or that you hear quite a lot about him when you learn about areas like personality and mental disorders.

Section summary

We have now seen that psychology has roots in both philosophy and biology, and we have covered all the schools of psychology that emerged during its early development as a discipline. We have seen that three of these essentially died out (structuralism, function-alism and Gestalt psychology), while the other two became main approaches that still exist today. Behaviourism became the most accepted approach within academic psychology for many years, whereas psychoanalysis became a major approach towards psychological matters, but existed largely outside of mainstream academic psychology. The next section will summarise developments in psychology since the 1950s (on our timeline), and will outline the way that psychology, as a discipline, looks today.

Quick test

Name the five early schools of psychology and briefly explain the ideas proposed by each of them.

Section 3

Psychology today

To understand psychology, you need to know how it looks as a discipline today and the more recent events that have shaped it.

The timeline displays three further developments in psychology following the behaviourist school of Watson and Skinner. The first is the 'humanistic' school of psychology. This came out of the work of Rogers and, like psychoanalysis, developed as a therapy to help people rather than an academic theory. It disputed the scientific method for studying humans (see Chapter 4), and also the behaviourist and psychoanalytic views that people are determined by their biology and/or the environment. Instead it saw people as possessing free will (see Chapter 5). The humanistic approach fitted in well with the social and cultural climate of the 1960s. Maslow described it as a 'third force', in addition to behaviourism and psychoanalysis, and hoped that it would unify these objective and subjective approaches into a 'holistic' psychology (Maslow was also influenced by Gestalt psychology). However, like psychoanalysis, humanism was never really accepted in mainstream academic psychology, although it has had a major impact on therapy for emotional disorders. We will describe and evaluate this approach in chapter 2.

CRUCIAL TIP

Graham (1986) states that 'eastern' psychology is much more humanist than the psychology we are familiar with in the West. It emphasises spiritual and subjective aspects of the individual, and is rooted in the tradition of mysticism rather than science. It is worth remembering that the psychology described in this book, and most psychology textbooks, is **western** psychology (i.e. dominated by Europe and the US). Other cultures might have very different versions of psychology, and different approaches might be dominant.

The next development was the 'cognitive revolution' in 1956. The idea of a revolution is actually a bit misleading. It has been said that history tends to be written by the winners, and the cognitive approach definitely 'won' in psychology, as it is dominant across much of the discipline today. Therefore, it makes sense for modern psychologists to see cognitivism as a revolutionary move away from behaviourism. In fact, the shift to cognitivism was probably too gradual to be a 'revolution'. Although behaviourism dominated psychology for 40 years or so, many were dissatisfied with its approach and not all went along with it. Köhler worked to keep Gestalt ideas alive in the US, and people like Piaget and Vygotsky carried out research in Europe and Russia that would eventually be taken up by cognitive psychologists. Finally, behaviourism didn't just disappear when cognitivism emerged. The two coexisted for several years.

The 'cognitive revolution' generally refers to a number of events in 1956 which can be seen as representing a culmination of dissatisfaction with behaviourism (see Figure 1.1). However, many psychologists trace the cognitive revolution to conferences in the US that happened before 1956. The cognitive approach is described in detail in chapter 2. For now, you just need to know that it was a return to studying mental processes, although in a very different way to the structuralist and functionalist schools, because cognitivism retained the very empirical, objective methods of the behaviourists.

Mainstream psychology today is shaped by its history, particularly by the behaviourist and cognitive approaches. Most mainstream researchers study behaviour and/or mental processes using the principles of the cognitive approach (content), and the scientific techniques proposed by behaviourism and cognitivism (method), as you can see from Zimbardo's (1992) definition that we looked at in section 1.

However, there is one further recent development that is worth mentioning. This is sometimes called the 'crisis' in social psychology, although it had implications beyond just social psychology. It occurred in the late 1960s and early 1970s, culminating in Harré and Secord's book (see figure 1.1). Rom Harré and others criticised mainstream psychology for its scientific methods and aimed to obtain 'objective truths' about human thought and behaviour. They referred to the mainstream as 'old paradigm' research, and proposed a 'new paradigm'. Their criticisms targeted:

- the methods used to study psychological phenomena in isolation, stripping them of their context;
- the idea that psychologists could be objective and bias-free.

These criticisms are considered in more depth in Chapter 4, and some of the alternative 'new paradigm' approaches are described at the end of Chapter 2.

However, despite the fact that the cognitive scientific approach to psychology has been attacked several times since the 1970s, it still remains the dominant perspective in the USA and the UK. This influences the way we study psychology (mostly with experiments and other such controlled techniques), and the way we view the object of study – people (generally as fairly passive 'subjects' who all function in very similar, quite mechanical ways, with behaviour and mental processes that can be broken down into separate parts, or variables, to study).

Chapter 2 describes the different approaches that are taken towards the study of psychology today. When you read these it is important to remember where they came from historically, and which are the dominant perspectives in psychology today. Most psychologists will come from one of these approaches, and use the principles and methods of that approach to study their particular topic area.

Psychologists study a whole range of different topics. Chapter 3 introduces you to some of the main sub-disciplines of psychology, dividing them up into 'pure' psychology (areas of academic psychological research) and 'applied' psychology (professions which use psychological techniques to deal with 'real-world' problems).

Figure 1.5 displays the different approaches and sub-disciplines (or topic areas) that you will cover in the next two chapters.

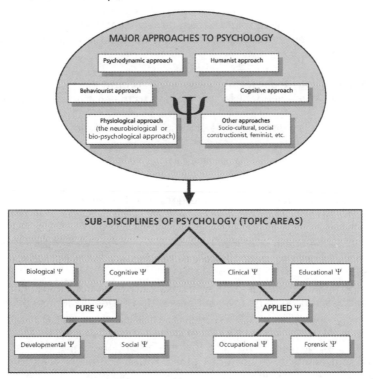

Figure 1.5 Approaches and sub-disciplines in psychology

CRUCIAL TIP

When you read other psychology textbooks, you will find that they all divide up the areas of psychology slightly differently, giving different numbers of branches of pure and applied psychology. Don't worry about this. Figure 1.5 just shows some of the main areas. Chapter 3 also mentions some further topics that other books/courses may include. The different sub-disciplines of psychology can be broken down in various different ways; as long as you know the main approaches and areas you should be fine.

Section summary

We have now brought psychology up to date. We can see that psychology today is dominated by the cognitive way of seeing people and the scientific way of doing research.

However, we also understand that there are alternative approaches to psychology such as humanist and new-paradigm approaches. Psychology today can be seen as a range of competing approaches to investigating similar psychological phenomena (the sub-disciplines).

Quick test

Outline the major developments in psychology since 1950.

Section 4

End of chapter assessment

Questions

These questions relate to the three assessment targets set at the beginning of this chapter. If you can answer them effectively you are in a good position to get good credit in assessments or examinations.

1. What can psychology today learn from studying its history?
2. What were the most important factors that led to the emergence of psychology as a discipline?
3. How did behaviourism differ from the other schools of psychology in the early twentieth century?

Answers

1. This is a very broad question. With questions like this, students generally make two common mistakes.

   - not reading the question properly – they might see the word 'history' and assume that they just need to write a history of psychology. This is not what the question asks for;
   - going too broad – there are so many things we can learn from studying the history of psychology you need to narrow your answer to consider just a few things.

   This latter point is vital. Don't be afraid to start the essay by saying that there are many things that psychology can learn, and that it is beyond the scope of the essay to cover them all, so it will focus on one or two main issues. You might want to consider the reasons we covered for studying the history of psychology in section 1 (from Jones and Elcock, 2001). You could briefly mention all of these and then focus on one of them (e.g. the fact it helps us to understand where current theories and debates have come from, the fact we can learn lessons from the past, or the fact that it is important to understand the context in which theories developed). You should use examples in your essay to support what you are saying. Explaining two or three in detail is, again, much better than trying to include lots of different examples. For instance, you could decide to focus on the behaviourist and cognitive revolutions, to explain how they have shaped the way in which psychology sees and studies people today. Alternatively, you could look at some 'mistakes' in the history of psychology that we need to learn from (for example, biases that were present in some past research – see Chapter 4). This is a question to come back to when you have finished the book, because you will have a better overall understanding by then. You wouldn't be expected to answer this straightaway in your psychology course!

If you get a coursework essay question like this and you are a bit worried about how to narrow your focus, write a brief structure of what you are planning to say and make an appointment with the module tutor to check it with them.

2. This is a question about the origins of psychology. You need to think back to 1879 and remind yourself how the climate back then enabled people like Wundt and James to form psychology departments as a separate academic discipline. Structure is really important for an essay like this. Use subheadings, and divide the essay up into various factors that were important. For example, you might want to consider the philosophical way of thinking at the time and the biological way of thinking separately (like I did). Or you might decide that three factors were important: the popularity of empirical research, the rediscovery of the study of mental processes in philosophy and the emergence of biology. You could give each of these a separate section in your essay. Remember to start off with an introduction saying how you are dividing it up, and finish with a conclusion, drawing it all together and explaining how psychology emerged.

3. Ah, a nice simple question! For this you just need to remind yourself what each of the early schools were about. You probably want to start with a brief explanation of behaviourism, then go through each of the other schools that were around at the time saying what they thought and how behaviourist psychology differed from this. Again, subsections are good for each school (structuralism, functionalism, Gestalt and psychoanalysis). A really good answer would display a historical awareness of how behaviourism developed out of functionalism. This would probably be an essay question. For a short answer question in an exam you might be asked to compare and contrast just two of the schools. Remember to say what their ideas were, how these were similar and different, and what their relative strengths and weaknesses were.

Section 5

Further reading and research

Most introductory psychology textbooks include a brief history of psychology adequate for a first-year course. However, these generally don't give much idea of the relationship between psychology and the rest of society. Such an understanding would be necessary for later modules.

For a nice, easy, introduction (with cartoons!) see:

Benson, N. C. and Grove, S. (1999) *Introducing Psychology.* London: Icon.

A very full, clear account of the origins of psychology, with lots of interesting stories, can be found in Chapter 5 of:

Colman, A. M. (1999) *What is psychology?* London: Routledge.

For an in-depth discussion of different ways of understanding the history of psychology and a critical analysis of how psychology has developed within its socio-cultural context, see:

Jones, D. and Elcock, J. (2001) *History and Theories of Psychology: A Critical Perspective.* London: Arnold.

Chapter 2
Theoretical approaches in psychology

Chapter summary

There are various different approaches in contemporary psychology. An approach is a perspective which involves certain assumptions about people: the way they function, which aspects of them are worthy of study and what methods are appropriate for undertaking this study. There may be several different theories within an approach, but they all share these common assumptions. Psychologists tend to engage with the topics they study from one of these approaches.

Chapter 1 gave you the historical background to each approach, explaining how the psychodynamic and behaviourist approaches came out of two of the early schools of psychology, while humanism and cognitivism emerged in the 1950s. It also showed you how cognitivism, and to some extent behaviourism, are major parts of academic psychology today, while psychodynamic and humanist psychology developed as therapies and do not tend to be accepted by mainstream psychology, although they do have some important influences on it. The physiological approach dates back to the biological research that pre-dated psychology as a discipline. This chapter outlines and evaluates each of the main approaches in psychology and some alternative approaches.

Assessment targets

Target 1: Describing the approaches
This chapter will enable you to describe each of the different approaches to psychology in terms of its content (what it considers worthy of study and the assumptions it makes about human beings) and its method (how it studies it). You will also be able to tie this knowledge in with what you learnt in the previous chapter about the historical background to each of the approaches. Question 1 at the end of the chapter tests your ability to describe the approaches.

Target 2: Evaluating the approaches
As well as being able to describe the approaches, you will also be able to 'evaluate' them. This means that you'll be able to assess their strengths and weaknesses. Question 2 at the end of the chapter tests your understanding of the pros and cons of each approach.

Target 3: Comparing the approaches
Finally, this chapter will show you how the different approaches compare to each other. You will learn the ways in which they are similar and different, and in what ways each approach is better or worse than the others. Question 3 at the end of the chapter tests how well you can compare and contrast the different approaches.

How will you be assessed on this?

You may well be asked to compare and contrast the approaches to psychology in exam and essay questions on introductory courses. This chapter covers the main theorists and theories within each approach that you would need to display knowledge of. It is also important to remember where each approach fits in to the history of psychology (see Chapter 1), and to know about key studies in each approach (covered here). All courses are likely to cover the behaviourist, cognitive and physiological approaches in depth. However, courses vary in the amount of space they give to the psychodynamic, humanist and other approaches, since these lie outside of mainstream psychology. You will need to be aware of these approaches, but check your own course to figure out the depth of knowledge that will be expected. For example, if there are lectures on therapies, it will be important to know more about the psychodynamic and humanist approaches. If you are at an institution like Loughborough, Gloucestershire, Bolton or Nottingham Trent, you will find there is more emphasis on critical and 'new paradigm' approaches than at some more traditional institutions.

Section 1

The psychodynamic approach

In Chapter 1, we learnt a little about where Freud's psychoanalysis came from, and saw that it is both a set of theories about personality and emotional development, and a form of therapy based on these theories. In this section we will summarise some of the key ideas and methods of psychoanalysis, and briefly explore other psychodynamic theories, before evaluating the contributions and limitations of this approach.

Explanation

--- CRUCIAL CONCEPT ---

The **psychodynamic approach** includes all the theories in psychology that see human functioning as based upon the interaction of drives and forces within the person, particularly unconscious conflict between the different structures of the personality. Freud's psychoanalysis (see chapter 1) was the original psychodynamic theory, but the psychodynamic approach as a whole includes all the other theories that were based on his ideas, e.g. Jung (1964), Adler (1927) and Erikson (1950).

--- CRUCIAL TIP ---

The words 'psychodynamic' and 'psychoanalytic' are often confused. Remember that Freud's theories were psychoanalytic, whereas the term 'psychodynamic' refers to both his theories and those of his followers.

Figure 2.1 outlines the main assumptions psychoanalysis makes about human behaviour, although it is important to note that Freud modified his theories over the course of his lifetime and other psychodynamic theorists adapted his ideas.

Freud's theories came from case studies of his therapeutic work with clients. Freud believed that people could be cured by making conscious their unconscious thoughts and motivations. He used various methods to gain access to the unconscious, the main ones being the following:

- **Free association** – the client says whatever comes into their mind, however seemingly irrelevant. If the client becomes 'blocked' talking about something, this indicates unconscious resistance. Unconscious ideas often come out in 'slips of the tongue' (hence the joke that a Freudian slip is when you say one thing and mean your mother!).

- **Dream analysis** – unconscious material also emerges in dreams, which the analyst can interpret.

- **Transference** – clients project and displace their thoughts and feelings onto the therapist.

Theory	Explanation
Unconscious mind	The mind is made up of unconscious, conscious and preconscious (thoughts available to conscious). The majority of our mind is the unconscious, containing hidden wishes, memories and fears. These come from childhood experiences (age 0–6) and biological instincts and drives (mostly sexual). The unconscious is not normally available to the conscious mind, although it does influence and direct our behaviour. The structure of the adult unconscious, once formed, is difficult to change.
Id, ego and superego	The personality consists of three main parts. The **id** is located in the unconscious mind. It is selfish and wants immediate gratification and pleasure (like a child). It contains the sexual instincts (libido) and aggressive instincts. The **ego** is the conscious, rational mind that develops during the first two years of life. It is realistic and protects individuals from the harm of always doing just what they want. The **superego** is the 'conscience' that develops by age 5, when the child adopts the values of the same-sex parent. It makes us feel guilty when we do wrong (what has been punished) and proud when we do right (what has been rewarded). It is partly conscious and partly unconscious.
Development	The personality goes through five stages of psychosexual development. Each focuses on a different source of pleasure. Failure to negotiate these stages (fixation at a stage) can cause later neuroses. • **Oral** (0–18 months) – satisfaction from sucking, eating, etc. • **Anal** (18–36 months) – toilet training occurs, anal region becomes source of satisfaction. • **Phallic** (3–6) – the Oedipus complex occurs: boys desire their mother and fear their father, who they believe may castrate them. The resolution is identification with the father. • **Latent** (6–puberty) – boys and girls are generally separate. • **Genital** (puberty–adulthood) – genitals are the main source of sexual pleasure.
Defence mechanisms	The id, ego and superego conflict. The ego uses defence mechanisms as strategies to reduce anxiety, e.g. • **repression** – pushing away unwanted ideas, keeping them out of the conscious mind; • **regression** – going back to an earlier stage of development; • **projection** attributing our qualities to someone else, e.g. a bossy person saying others are bossy; • **displacement** – diverting energy into another activity, e.g. taking anger at boss out on the dog; • **denial** – refusing to accept the existence of a threat, e.g. a sick person denying they are really ill.

Figure 2.1 The major principles of psychoanalytic theory (Freud, 1856–1939)

---- CRUCIAL STUDY ----

In 1909, Freud wrote a paper based on a case study of a five-year-old boy, little Hans, who was afraid of horses. In the paper he analyses Hans through correspondence with his father and direct psychoanalysis and finds the following:

- Hans likes getting into bed with his mother.
- Hans has been told that if he touches his 'widdler' (penis), it will be cut off.
- Hans saw a horse fall over, which scared him; he describes the black bits around its mouth in particular.
- Hans had a dream where he took a crumpled giraffe away from a big giraffe and sat on it.
- Towards the end of his phobia Hans had one fantasy of being married to his mother and playing with their children, and another of having his 'widdler' replaced with a bigger one.

Freud concludes that Hans is going through the Oedipus complex (Figure 2.1), and that the phobia is caused by hidden conflicts in his unconscious. The horse represents his father (the black bits around its mouth looks like a moustache), as does the big giraffe in his dream (the crumpled one represents his mother). Freud asks Hans 'when the horse fell down did you think of your daddy?' and Hans says 'Perhaps. Yes it's possible' (p. 213). Hans is helped through psychoanalysis to express his fears and wishes and is therefore able to resolve these conflicts.

Evaluation

Freud's theories affected many later thinkers. Other psychodynamic theorists who were strongly influenced include the following:

- Carl Jung – proposed a more spiritual theory, with the idea that humans have a 'collective unconscious' based on the experiences of our ancestors and reflected in cultural myths and symbols. He also saw people as being born with an 'introvert' or 'extravert' personality type (depending on whether they are mainly concerned with their internal world or with the outside world).
- Alfred Adler – who saw human motivation as mostly conscious, and proposed birth order as being important in the development of personality.
- Melanie Klein – who pioneered 'play therapy' to tap into young children's unconscious (see Axline, 1990, for an account of this). Bowlby's 'attachment theory' of childhood development developed from Klein's ideas. He proposed that children have evolved to attach to one person in particular, usually the mother.
- Erik Erikson – who trained with Anna Freud (Freud's daughter) and proposed the less sexual 'psychosocial' stages of development which cover the whole lifespan, not just early childhood.

Rogers (humanist therapist) and Perls (Gestalt therapist) were also trained psychoanalysts. Therefore the psychodynamic approach has impacted on the therapies used by many psychotherapists, psychiatrists and clinical psychologists.

The psychodynamic approach has had a very wide influence on western culture, especially in the analysis of literature and art. Many psychodynamic words and concepts are now part of our daily language (e.g. ego, defensive, repressed, unconscious, extravert), often being regarded as 'common sense' and shaping the way we think about our own psychological functioning.

CRUCIAL TIP

Before we look at weakness of the approach, look at the crucial study again, and come up with your own criticisms.

As we saw in Chapter 1, academic psychologists are generally not keen to embrace psychodynamics. Here are just a few of the criticisms that have been levelled at the theories of Freud and his followers. Most are based on their 'unscientific' nature (see Chapter 4). The theories were criticised for being:

- **Unfalsifiable.** Karl Popper (1959) pointed out that many of the claims cannot be disproved, and science should always be refutable (see the hypethetico-deductive method, Chapter 4).
- **Methodologically poor.** Hans Eysenck (1985) and others have pointed out that Freud's ideas were based on a small number of case studies (only about twelve were published). Can these really be generalised to all human behaviour? Is Hans representative of all children? Also, analysts may influence what clients say.
- **Subjective.** Much psychodynamic therapy depends on the interpretation of the particular analyst.
- **Incorrect.** Later evidence has shown several theories to be faulty. There is little evidence for Freud's stages of psychosexual development. Biological evidence fails to support his models of the mind. There is evidence that many emotional problems are not rooted in early childhood experiences.
- **Biased.** Freud's ideas have been criticised as being sexist, and many argue that they really only apply to the Viennese people who Freud was studying around 1900. Gender, culture and historical bias are all present in the theories (see Chapter 4). This is a helpful reminder that it is always worth considering the social context in which theories are proposed.

Proponents of psychodynamics would argue that, although many of the ideas cannot be precisely measured, they are appropriate for capturing the complex nature of human experience and action (Stevens, 1995). It is also important to remember that disproving some of the separate hypothesis suggested by psychodynamics does not mean that the whole approach is wrong,

---
CRUCIAL TIP

The Psychologist magazine published a special issue in December 2001 containing some positive evaluations of Freud's theories in the light of modern research. This is well worth reading to balance the criticisms you will find in many textbooks.

Section summary

In this section we have seen that the main ideas in psychoanalysis are the unconscious mind and the influence of instinctual sexual drives and early childhood experiences. We have looked at the methods and contributions of the psychodynamic approach, and seen that mainstream psychology generally does not accept it because it is seen as unscientific. It is helpful to compare the crucial study in this section to that in the next section which outlines a different (behaviourist) approach to phobias.

Quick test

Briefly explain each of Freud's main theories. How convincing do you find each of them?

Section 2

The behaviourist approach

We introduced the behaviourist school in chapter 1 and saw that the approach limited the content of psychological study to observable behaviour and used the method of objective experimentation. In this section, we cover some of the more specific theories and research in behaviourism, and evaluate their contributions and limitations.

Explanation

To recap, the basic assumption that behaviourists make about humans is that virtually all behaviours are caused by learned relationships between a stimulus (S) that excites the sense organs, and a response (R) which is a reaction to the stimulus. For example, seeing a snake (S) and running away (R), smelling a burger (S) and eating it (R). This is such a vital part of behaviourism that alternative names for the approach are 'learning theory' and 'stimulus-response (S-R) psychology'.

The main behaviourist method was the controlled experiment (see Chapter 4), since behaviourists placed great importance on objective, empirical research. The behaviourists were strongly on the 'nurture' side of the nature–nurture debate (see Chapter 5), since they saw human behaviour as learnt rather than inherited.

Let's look in more detail at the main behaviourist theories of learning: classical conditioning and operant conditioning, and the studies they are based on.

Watson and the other early behaviourists were strongly influenced by the work of the Russian physiologist, Pavlov, on classical conditioning. Pavlov trained dogs to salivate when he rang a bell. Salivation is a reflex response in dogs when they see food. Pavlov rang a bell whenever dogs were given food. After several repetitions of this the dogs began to salivate whenever they heard the bell, even if the food was not there (see Figure 2.2).

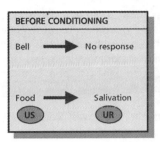
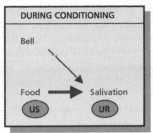
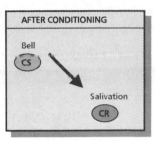

Figure 2.2 Pavlov's classical conditionng

An unconditioned stimulus (US) leads to an unconditioned response (UR). When the unconditioned stimulus (US) is paired with another stimulus, this stimulus eventually produces the response on its own, and is then called the conditioned stimulus (CS), which produces a conditioned response (CR).

────── CRUCIAL CONCEPT ──────

Classical conditioning occurs when we make an association between a neutral stimulus and a stimulus that reliably produces a response, so that the neutral stimulus comes to produce the same response.

────── CRUCIAL TIP ──────

The comedian, Eddie Izzard, does a sketch in which he questions what would have happened if Pavlov had carried out his studies on cats. He proposes that cats would have refused to comply and it would have ended up with them ringing the bell and Pavlov eating the food! What do you think would have happened if Pavlov had used cats? What about humans?

────── CRUCIAL STUDY ──────

Watson and Rayner (1920) carried out a study to demonstrate that Pavlov's research could be applied to humans. They investigated whether emotional responses, like fear, could be classically conditioned. They took an emotionally stable nine-month-old boy called little Albert (no relation to little Hans!). First they established that Albert was not frightened of rats, his natural response was to play with them. Then they used classical conditioning to train him to fear rats. Children are startled by loud noises, so they struck a steel bar with a hammer just behind Albert's head as the unconditioned stimulus. By repeatedly pairing this with the presentation of a rat, over several days, they conditioned Albert to fear rats; he began to withdraw from them and sometimes cry. He showed similar responses to other animals and furry things, but not to things like building blocks (see Figure 2.3).

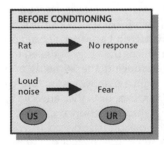
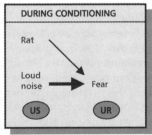
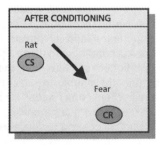

Figure 2.3 Watson's classical conditioning of emotional response

The behaviourist approach would propose that most phobias come about in a similar way to this. For example, a spider-phobic might learn to be scared of spiders because their parent always screams when they see a spider, or because they hear about spiders in the context of scary stories. The parent's reaction or story is the unconditioned stimulus that provokes the fear response, which eventually becomes the conditioned response to the spider alone.

Other than Watson, the most influential behaviourist psychologist was Skinner. He investigated what he called operant conditioning, the learning process where rewarding a response leads to learning. He put animals in a controlled environment known as the 'Skinner box'. He found that he could train rats to press a lever or pigeons to peck a certain spot if he rewarded them for doing so with food. The stimulus (reward) strengthened the response, making it more likely to happen again. Skinner also found that punishment (such as electric shocks) weakened the response.

CRUCIAL CONCEPT

Operant (or **instrumental**) **conditioning** is a process of stimulus-response learning in which an action (operant) is learnt through reinforcement. Reinforcement can be positive (rewarding the action with a pleasant stimulus) or negative (punishing the action with an unpleasant stimulus, or removing the reward).

From Skinner's research we get the joke that magicians pull rabbits out of hats, psychologists pull habits out of rats.

Evaluation

We saw in Chapter 1 that the behaviourist approach improved psychology's scientific status, since it proposed clear hypotheses that could be tested by controlled, systematic experimentation. Whether this was positive or negative depends on your view of whether psychology should be scientific (see Chapter 4). Whatever the case, the methods of behaviourism became an integral part of psychology.

Conditioning has been used to explain aspects of memory and language development, and current 'learning theory' in cognitive psychology is an extension of the work of Pavlov and Skinner. Also, Bandura's (1977) 'social learning theory' built on the original behaviourist work to account for more complex human behaviour. Bandura argued that children learn new behaviour through imitating other people (observational learning). This has been used to support the view that media violence can lead to aggression. Bandura investigated this in the famous 'Bobo doll' experiment where children imitated an adult they had seen hitting the doll in a film, particularly if the adult was rewarded. Social learning theory has also put forward an explanation of gender development: gender-appropriate behaviour is reinforced in children through rewards (often praise), and children model the behaviour of same-sex adults.

The other major contribution of behaviourism is 'behaviour therapy', which is a group of therapeutic techniques based on the idea that abnormal behaviour comes about through conditioning, and can be removed in the same way. **Desensitisation therapy** is based on classical conditioning (Lang and Lazovik, 1963). It gradually reduces the bond between the conditioned stimulus and the response (fear) by slowly introducing the stimulus and getting the phobic to relax. For example a spider-phobic might be shown a picture of spider, then a small spider in a tank, then a larger spider in a tank, etc., until they are able to relax even with a tarantula on the back of their neck! **Aversion therapy** reduces unwanted behaviours like addictions by pairing the thing the person is addicted to with something that gives an unpleasant response (e.g. putting a substance in alcoholic drinks that makes the person feel sick). **Behaviour modification** uses operant conditioning, rewarding people for positive behaviour so that they will behave in that way more often. Other behavioural techniques you might want to read up on are **flooding** and **biofeedback**. Behavioural techniques have also been used in education and the work-place, both attempting to improve performance through reinforcement (see Chapter 3).

The behaviourist approach has been criticised for being:

- **Mechanistic and oversimplified** – it ignores mental processes, or reinterprets them as just types of behaviour. Watson saw emotions as the secretion of glands and thinking as the movement of vocal chords without actual speech. However, studies have found that people can still think even when their vocal chords are paralysed! Social learning theory has also been criticised for not including internal thought processes.
- **Limited** – not everything can be accounted for by simple learning (e.g. new or creative behaviour, more complex behaviours).
- **'Environmentally deterministic'** – it sees no role for biological factors in human behaviour (see chapter 5).
- **Over-reliant on animal research** – such research has been questioned in terms of ethics (see Chapter 3) and to what extent findings from animals apply to humans. For example, humans have language, so, unlike a rat, they will stop pressing a lever if they are told that no more rewards will be given.
- **Shallow** – behavioural therapies have been criticised from treating the symptoms but ignoring the underlying causes of problems (also see Chapter 3 for ethical problems).

Section summary

This section has covered the basic learning theories of the behaviourist approach, and has examined some of the applications of behaviourism and its weaknesses. Section 4 will explore the relationship between cognitivism and behaviourism. Cognitivists have criticised the S-R theory for ignoring the mental processes that come between the stimulus and the response. However, one of the most recent trends in cognitive psychology, connectionism, is founded on several principles of association that originated in behaviourism.

Quick test

Explain classical conditioning and operant conditioning. Give one practical application of each.

Section 3

The humanistic approach

Like the psychodynamic approach, the humanist approach initially developed as a therapy, and humanist theories are not accepted in mainstream academic psychology, although they have had a marked influence on clinical psychology and counselling. This section explains the approach, along with some of its contributions, and the reasons for its limited acceptance.

Explanation

As we saw in Chapter 1, the humanist approach sees people as having free will rather than being driven by unconscious forces or external reinforcement. In this way, it differs from the other two approaches covered so far. Humanists share the optimistic assumptions that people are free to choose their own destiny and that they endeavour to achieve their potential for psychological growth within the confines of any individual limitations (see Chapter 5 for more on free will).

Humanists tend to reject the scientific method as inappropriate for studying people. They dispute the idea that detached, objective observers can understand human behaviour, arguing that only the person themselves can explain their behaviour; they are the expert, not the researcher or therapist. Humanists favour the method of 'phenomenology' in both therapy and research.

CRUCIAL CONCEPT

Phenomenology is the study of phenomena as perceived by the individual. It emphasises the subjective experience of the person perceiving events and their self-reports.

Humanism also rejects the idea that human behaviour can be seen as collections of separate mechanisms. Such views are held by many scientific psychologists, who study people in fragmented ways, separating out aspects of thought or behaviour (reductionism – see Chapter 5). Humanists argue that we need to study the person as a whole.

CRUCIAL CONCEPT

Humanism is the approach within psychology that emphasises the whole person as a free individual who strives to maximise their potential.

We will now briefly look at the key ideas of the two best-known humanists: Carl Rogers and Abraham Maslow.

Rogers' theory of personality proposed that people were innately good and unique, with a basic need to be respected by others. People are born with an 'actualising tendency' (a drive to develop into mature, healthy human beings). Their sense of themselves is constantly changing, based on their experiences (this contrasts with most other theorists who see the 'self' as the fixed part of our personality).

Rogers believed that the self had two components: the perceived self (how we see ourselves) and the ideal self (how we think we should be). Good psychological health and self-esteem come when these are well matched. If they are not, we get psychological problems. Rogers saw a lot of our problems as coming from 'conditions of worth', which are the messages we get as we grow up about how we should behave in order to gain love and approval. These messages mean that our ideal self is hard to achieve. For example, we might learn that it is important to be very attractive or intelligent, and not feel that we measure up to this.

Based on these ideas, Rogers developed 'client-centred therapy'. In this, people are perceived as having the power and motivation to help themselves; the therapist is just a 'facilitator', creating an environment for growth through the following behaviours:

- empathy (listening and displaying understanding);
- congruence (being honest and open);
- unconditional positive regard for the client;
- being non-directive and non-judgemental (not pushing the client or making judgements about them).

This helps clients to understand themselves better and get more control over their situation (empowerment). Rogers also used 'group therapy' where clients helped each other.

Abraham Maslow shared many of Rogers' ideas (the actualising tendency and the importance of self-awareness). He proposed an inborn 'hierarchy of needs', arguing that we have to satisfy the lower needs (or deficiencies) before we can strive for the higher motivations (and grow). 'Self-actualisation' is the pinnacle, the 'peak experience' where we reach our full potential, everything we are capable of being (see Figure 2.4).

Figure 2.4 Maslow's hierarchy of needs

Evaluation

Rogers' 'client-centred' therapy is the most significant contribution of the humanistic approach. This had a huge impact on psychotherapy in general, and many clinical psychologists and counsellors today use it as the basis of their therapy. The emphasis on the personal qualities of the therapist contributed to the development of the counselling profession. Counsellors do not have to have a background in medicine or psychology. Counselling skills can also be taught in other professions (e.g. business, education, social work). The 'recovery movement', including organisations like Alcoholics Anonymous (AA), use many humanistic ideas (Malim and Birch, 1998).

Rogers also developed techniques for measuring the progress of therapy (e.g. Q sort), suggesting that it should be subjected to research scrutiny. This was a vital contribution because therapists need to know whether their methods are actually effective (see Chapter 3).

CRUCIAL TIP

You might also have noticed that humanistic ideas seem more relevant to your own life than much of psychology. They cover issues that are central to our lives. Students starting out in psychology often expect it to be more like the humanist approach. We will consider this issue more when we look at 'psychology and common sense' in Chapter 5.

The humanistic approach has been criticised in similar ways to the psychodynamic approach for being 'unscientific':

- **lack of empirical research**: the theories come from Rogers' and Maslow's observations of human nature;

- **difficult to test**: the terminology is not clearly defined.

Also:

- **limited therapy**: humanistic therapy may be limited with people who are not motivated or seriously disturbed;
- **culture-bias**: Maslow's hierarchy of needs has been criticised for being based on Western, individualistic values (see Chapter 4).

Section summary

The humanistic approach can be seen as providing an important counterbalance to the deterministic, scientific approaches that have dominated psychology. It has had a significant impact on counselling and psychotherapy. However, few mainstream academic psychologists adopt this approach today.

Quick test

List the key ways in which the humanistic approach differs from other psychological approaches.

Section 4

The cognitive approach

In Chapter 1 we saw how the cognitive approach to psychology emerged out of dissatisfaction with behaviourism. This section outlines the way this approach views humans and the techniques it uses to study them, along with its strengths and limitations. Chapter 3 gives more information about cognitive psychology as a sub-discipline of psychology and the areas which cognitive psychologists study.

Explanation

The cognitive approach disputes the behaviourist notion that human behaviour can be understood in terms of learnt associations between a stimulus and a response. Cognitive psychologists argue that it is necessary to study what comes between these, i.e. mental processes. These internal events are often called 'mediators' (see Figure 2.5).

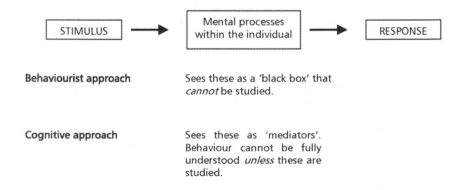

Figure 2.5 Behaviourist and cognitive approaches to mental processes

For example, earlier we used the examples of seeing a snake (S) and running away (R), or smelling a burger (S) and eating it (R). The cognitive approach would say that we could only fully understand those behaviours by understanding the mediating mental processes, or cognitions. With the snake, mediators could be: the perception of the snake by the visual system, memories of previous encounters with snakes and the fact they might be dangerous, emotions such as fear, problem solving as we decide what to do. With the burger, some mediators could be: the perception of the smell linked to the memory that burgers taste good, and the language involved in asking for the burger.

In addition to emphasising the importance of mental processes, cognitive psychologists took up a new model for understanding them. People had often tried to understand the mind by comparing it to other systems. Analogies made in the past included clocks and telephone exchanges. Cognitive psychologists latched onto the electronic computer, which was developing at the time. They argued that computers are similar to human brains since they also have inputs and outputs, memory stores and data processing systems. Therefore, the brain can be examined by comparing it to a computer.

So cognitive psychologists saw the brain as an 'information processor'. Their main goal was to produce models of how this processor might operate, to explain how the various cognitions work (language, memory, etc.) These models were necessary because physiological research was not yet advanced enough to directly uncover the functions of the brain.

CRUCIAL CONCEPT

The cognitive approach sees internal mental processes (cognitions) as vital in understanding human behaviour. Such processes include memory, perception, problem-solving and language. These are modelled according to the 'information processor', computer analogy of the brain.

Unlike the other approaches, there are no one or two main figures in the cognitive approach. Key people in its early development include Simon, Miller, Bruner, Neisser, Broadbent and the linguist Chomsky.

Cognitive psychologists kept the experimental, controlled methods of behaviourism, but applied them to cognitions. Since these could not be studied directly, two main techniques were developed.

- **Experimental cognitive psychology.** This studies individuals in controlled laboratory experiments. For example, to study how memory works, we might give people a list of words to memorise, then give them a test where we flash words up on a computer screen and ask them to say whether they were present on the original list or not. In this way we could study which type of words are remembered most easily, whether the order of words on the list is important, whether there is an impact of giving them another task to do between seeing the list and doing the memory test, etc. This helps us to model how memory works.

- **Cognitive science.** This involves producing 'artificially intelligent' computer programs which imitate the processes of the brain (so the same inputs give the same outputs). We can then assume that the processes in the brain work in similar ways to these programs. Some cognitive scientists try to model complex human behaviours like language and chess-playing. Others argue that we should start by creating robotic models of simple creatures like insects, capable of basic behaviours like moving around obstacles, then build up from there in a way analogous to evolution.

Cognitive neuropsychologists and cognitive neuroscientists also use the cognitive approach (combined with the physiological approach), but study the brain more directly (see section 4).

Evaluation

Cognitivism is an approach with its own explanations and methods, but particular subject areas are also fundamental. These are the topics investigated by the sub-discipline of cognitive psychology (see Chapter 3). However, the cognitive approach has also been adopted by many other areas of study.

- In developmental psychology there has been much interest in children's cognitive development (acquiring mathematical and linguistic abilities, etc.). Developmental psychologists embraced the theories of Piaget, who researched this area before the emergence of the cognitive approach (see Chapter 3).

- In social psychology focus has turned towards 'social cognition', the idea that how we behave in social situations depends on our cognitions about ourselves and others. This area studies how people think about themselves and the groups they belong to, as well as how they form opinions and make judgements about others (see Chapter 3).

- Like all the other approaches mentioned so far, there is a type of therapy based on the cognitive approach. Beck's 'cognitive therapy' sees emotional disorders as rooted in negative spirals of thought and emotion that people get into. The therapy involves clients testing these faulty thought patterns and replacing them with more helpful ones (see Chapter 3).

Eysenck (2000) states that the greatest strength of the cognitive approach is its various rigorous methods. Hypotheses can be tested in human experiments (cognitive psychology), computer models (cognitive science) and in brain studies (cognitive neuropsychology and cognitive neuroscience). If these methods all confirm a theory, we can be much more confident about it. Also, the cognitive approach has encouraged discussion between psychology and other disciplines such as computer science, biology and linguistics.

Although cognitivism remains the dominant approach in psychology, there are problems with it:

- **Artificial research.** It doesn't study real people using their mental processes in real situations because it is often difficult to test theories about cognition in natural settings. This means that results of experiments may not be applicable to everyday life (see Chapter 4). People do not function as isolated information processors, but within a rich environment of social interactions. Cognitive psychologists always have to grapple with the trade-off between methodological rigour and artificiality.

- **Lack of integration between the different 'cognitive theories'.** There is no one coherent framework linking cognitive theories of memory, thinking, etc. to cognitive theories of emotion in clinical psychology, or cognitive theories in social psychology like social cognition and cognitive dissonance (Malim and Birch, 1998).

- **The computer analogy of the brain.** Human thinking differs from computers. There are often many different processes going on at once in the brain (at the moment you may be reading, breathing, feeling hungry and wondering what to have for tea!). Also, human thinking is often imprecise because it is hard to keep many different pieces of information in mind (we would take hours or even days to do some of the complex mathematical problems that a computer can do in seconds; we forget and computers do not). Just because computers and humans produce similar outputs does not mean they were arrived at in the same way. It is important to remember that the computer analogy is just a metaphor and, as such, is limited in explaining human behaviour (see Searle, 1980).

- **Computer modelling.** Related to the previous point, there is much debate about whether cognitive scientists can ever really model human mental processes with computers. Computers do not have feelings, emotions or morals outside Hollywood movies, and many argue that they never will. Computer programs also do not show us what might be happening in the brain on a moment-by-moment basis.

These latter two points are addressed by the most recent development in cognitivism towards 'connectionism'. The connectionist metaphor of mental processes has now, to a large extent, taken the place of the computer metaphor.

───────────────── CRUCIAL CONCEPT ─────────────────

The **connectionist**, or 'brain'/'neural', model of mental processes sees them as simplified brain circuits whose behaviour can be understood mathematically.

The computer metaphor was 'algorithmic', meaning that it modelled mental processes on diagrams or flow charts. Each process was seen as a set of serial stages, one following another. 'A' had to be completed before 'B' could happen, then 'C', etc. For example, the algorithm for making a cup of tea might be: fill kettle with water, switch on kettle, wait for kettle to boil, put tea bag in mug, pour on water from kettle, add milk. This is roughly how computer programs work.

Connectionism proposes that the brain functions differently to this because it has many processors operating in parallel. We may be going through different parts of the 'making a cup of tea' process simultaneously, for example boiling the water, finding the mug and getting the tea bag and milk. At the same time we will probably be undertaking many other mental processes such as listening to the radio, planning an evening out, feeling frustrated about the long queue at the supermarket and putting the shopping away.

So the connectionist model sees the brain as a richly interconnected set of processors or neurons. Information is shared across vast networks of these processors (neural networks) and the various networks operate in parallel. So, for example, one memory is not located in one neuron but is distributed across a network of neurons. This explains why, when we remember a childhood picnic, we get a whole complex memory of tastes, smells, textures, sounds, sights, emotions, etc. Remembering one aspect of the picnic, such as the pattern on the rug that your parents always took, will inevitably trigger all the related memories about how the rug felt and smelt, the picnic in general, the trip there and back and other events around that time. This can be explained by the connectionist model of the brain, which sees it as networks of interconnected neurons.

The connectionist metaphor is preferable to the computer metaphor because it can model the complexity of human thought. It suggests that new information is not stored randomly, as on a computer, but at locations close to existing information that is related in meaning. This helps to explain the way that humans learn; for example, if we are learning to drive and learn something new, such as how to reverse, this will be stored near the other skills and knowledge related to driving, so we can integrate it with these and access it easily in the appropriate situation. Connectionism also explains how the human brain can continue to function when damaged. The destruction of some neurons does not destroy the whole interconnected network. Finally, connectionism is advantageous because it seems to be closer than previous models to the way the brain actually functions on a biological level. It makes important links between behaviour, cognition and neurophysiology. The last chapter of the Crucial Study Text on cognitive psychology covers connectionism in much greater depth.

Section summary

Here and in Chapter 1 we have seen that cognitivism is the dominant approach in psychology today, and that it uses scientific methods to study mental processes, initially seeing the brain as an 'information processor', rather like a computer, but more recently seeing it as a network of neural connections (connectionism). The cognitivist approach has helped psychology's standing as a science, but has marginalised approaches that see humans in other ways (e.g. humanism and other more 'social science' approaches to psychology).

Quick test

Explain how the cognitive approach sees mental processes and how it studies them.

Section 5

The physiological approach

The physiological approach to psychology investigates psychological functioning by studying biological processes directly. As we saw above, this can be compatible with the cognitive approach. In this section we briefly outline and evaluate the physiological approach. Chapter 3 gives more information about biological psychology as a sub-discipline of psychology and the areas which biological psychologists study.

Explanation

CRUCIAL CONCEPT

The **physiological approach** assumes that all human behaviour is related to physiological processes.

This approach dates back to the early physiologists of behaviour such as Ernst Weber and Wernicke (see Chapter 1). Physiological psychologists study a range of different areas of human functioning with various methods. They really just share the assumption of the importance of biological factors and a commitment to the scientific method. Here are some of the physiological factors that are investigated, and the methods for investigating them:

- **Localisation of function.** Continuing the early work of Broca and Wernike, many cognitive neuropsychologists have studied people with defects in particular areas of the brain to discover which areas of the brain are responsible for which functions. For example, the fact that some brain-damaged patients can understand language but can't use it coherently (in speech or writing) suggests that these two functions are based in different areas of the brain. Cognitive neuroscientists also study brain functions, but generally in 'normal' brains, using imaging techniques (such as PET (positron emission tomography) and MRI (magnetic resonance imaging)) to see which areas are active when people are performing different types of tasks. Brain areas have also been studied by electrically stimulating areas and seeing how people (or animals) respond.

- **Biochemistry.** Physiological psychologists also study the activity of neurons (nerve cells) within the brain. These are the cells that transmit information. The neurotransmitter chemicals that pass between the neurons have been studied to determine what they do. For example, the neurotransmitter serotonin is involved in arousal and mood. People with clinical depression may have too little active serotonin passing between the neurons in their brains; therefore they are often prescribed drugs like Prozac which extend the serotonin activity. Other important chemicals include acetylcholine (involved in memory) and dopamine (involved in movement and attention).

- **The role of heredity in behaviour.** Some physiological psychologists investigate genetic influences on behaviour, whether genes pass on behavioural characteristics like intelligence or personality in the same way they do physical ones like eye colour. Some psychologists have studied identical twins who were reared apart. Identical twins have identical genes; therefore, if they have very similar behaviours it seems likely that these are genetic. Such studies have found that some types of schizophrenia may have a genetic basis. Other 'evolutionary' psychologists follow Darwin's theories (see Chapter 1) to investigate the ways in which certain behaviours have evolved in animals, often suggesting generalisations to human behaviour (e.g. in the areas of altruism, aggression and mating behaviour). The study of natural animal behaviour is also known as 'comparative psychology' (comparisons are made to human behaviour).

- **Psychoimmunology.** Physiological psychologists have found that mental states can influence physical health. For example, stress has been found to affect the immune system, possibly leaving us more open to diseases like colds and cancer.

Evaluation

The physiological approach has accumulated a lot of valuable evidence, and this has led to applications such as the development of psychoactive drugs to treat mental disorders.

However, it has been criticised for being 'reductionist' (explaining all behaviour in terms of the actions of neurones and chemicals). Actually, many physiological psychologists take a more 'interactionist' approach, seeing physiological factors as contributing to behaviour but not necessarily determining it. For example, just because we know that serotonin has a role in depression doesn't mean that we assume that low serotonin uptake **causes** depression. It could be that one reaction to negative events in life is a decrease in serotonin uptake. In most areas of psychology, it is limiting to propose biological causes without taking account of the role of external factors.

Evolutionary psychology has been heavily criticised. To take the example of gender, evolutionary psychologists have suggested that men and women are different now because they needed to be different for survival in primitive times. Men are more aggressive and women more nurturing because survival of the species was optimised by men doing the hunting and women looking after the children. Also men are more naturally promiscuous than women because it made evolutionary sense for them to have several mates to maximise their chances of passing on their genes, whereas it made more sense for females to choose one male who was strong and whose children were more likely to survive. Critics argue that this evolutionary psychology portrays male aggression and sexual exploitation as natural, unavoidable and even desirable. Also, it is very unlikely that there is a single gene for hair colour, let alone a complex behaviour like these, and no genetic evidence have yet been found to support these arguments. Evolutionary psychologists assume a lot about how people lived in prehistoric times, without much evidence. Finally, evolutionary psychology has been criticised for underestimating the role of culture in human behaviour. There is much evidence that the differences and similarities between men and women vary across cultures, and that societal notions about 'masculine' and 'feminine' behaviour have a major influence on how men and women behave (see Figure 5.7 in Chapter 5 for a popular example of evolutionary psychology).

Chapter 5 contains a more detailed discussion of these issues of reductionism, determinism and the nature/nurture debate.

Section summary

The physiological approach focuses on the biological bases of behaviour, studying them in a number of ways, and helping us to understand the part played by brain and body processes in our behaviour, as well as the possible involvement of inherited characteristics.

Quick test

Describe some of the different areas of physiological research in psychology.

Section 6

Other approaches to psychology

Eysenck (1998) states that numerous other approaches have become influential in psychology during the latter part of the twentieth century. However, many of these are of such recent origin that it is hard to assess their long-term significance. Here we will briefly overview three of these more social and critical approaches to psychology: the socio-cultural approach, social constructionism and feminist psychology.

Some books on psychology consider the socio-cultural perspective to be an approach in its own right (e.g. Benson and Grove, 1999); however, many do not. This approach is really the flip side of the physiological approach, since it explains human behaviour in terms of the external environment rather than internal biology.

--- CRUCIAL CONCEPT ---

Socio-cultural approaches study the way in which human functioning and behaviour is influenced by external factors including social relationships (friends, family, workmates), social class, religion, and culture in general. Socialisation is the process of learning the social rules or 'norms' of our culture.

The socio-cultural assumptions and methods are close to those used in sociology and anthropology. Examples of socio-cultural research might be:

- cross-cultural studies, which look at differences in behaviour across cultures (e.g. studies have found that some cultures have quite different gender norms to ours, with women more dominant and aggressive and/or men more passive and social. This suggests that gender-appropriate behaviour is not inbuilt);
- observational or interview studies on particular groups within a culture (e.g. psychologists have joined religious cults or gangs to study the behaviour of members of these 'subcultures').

The socio-cultural approach can be criticised in the opposite way to the physiological approach: for explaining everything in terms of social factors and not considering biological ones.

A more extreme version of the socio-cultural approach is known as 'social constructionism'. Social constructionist ideas dominate most of the other 'social sciences' (e.g. sociology, cultural studies). However, many psychologists are hardly aware of them, probably because they challenge the dominant objective, scientific ways of studying human behaviour. In psychology, this perspective stems from the 'new paradigm' psychology that we covered in Chapter 1.

Social constructionists tend to share the following assumptions (Burr, 1995):

- A critical stance towards taken-for-granted knowledge – we should constantly question the way that we understand the world rather than assuming that we know the truth based on our objective observations. For example, constructionists question the ways in which we categorise people (by age, gender, culture etc.), assuming that these are naturally occurring differences between people. They may just be distinctions that we have given importance, and perhaps we could equally well have chosen to emphasise differences, for example, between tall and short people.

- Historical and cultural specificity – the ways we understand the world depend on where and when we live. For example, now we tend to class people as children, teenagers or adults. In the past, people were seen as going straight from childhood to adulthood, without the 'teenage' years in between.

- Knowledge is sustained by social processes – our common ways of understanding the world are constructed and sustained in our interactions (or discourses) with the social world (e.g. watching TV, gossiping with friends). Certain constructions are dominant in our society, so we are more likely to take these up.

- Knowledge and social action go together – different ways of understanding the world bring with them different ways of acting. For example, when homosexuality was seen as a crime, people were imprisoned for it; when it was seen as a sickness, they were treated; now it is seen as an acceptable sexuality and same-sex relationships are accepted, to some extent (although not as much as heterosexual relationships, which are still our 'dominant' way of seeing sexuality).

CRUCIAL CONCEPT

Social constructionism is the approach that sees social reality as constructed between people rather than being an objective phenomenon.

CRUCIAL TIP

To understand some of the ideas here more fully, take the example of something that we often take for granted: romantic love. Go through each of the assumptions above. How might we question the 'natural-ness' of romantic love? Is it historically and culturally specific? How might our understanding of it be sustained by social processes? What social actions might result from our way of seeing it? You might want to think about how love is portrayed in movies and magazines, and how it is understood by other cultures, like those based on arranged marriages.

So social constructionism does not attempt to study 'reality', but rather how we construct meanings of the world. In Chapters 1 and 4 we cover the criticisms that the 'new paradigm' social constructionist approach makes of traditional psychological methods, and the methods it uses. Social constructionists also see many psychological concepts (like intelligence, personality, attitudes and mental illness) as being constructed, in part, by psychology itself. As you can imagine, some psychologists aren't too happy about the suggestion that the things they study are not naturally occurring phenomena! For more about how some of these ideas apply to psychology, see section 2 of Chapter 4.

Critics of social constructionism have argued that some things **do** naturally occur, independent of our actions. Others have criticised the complexity of some of the ideas in social constructionism, and the tendency to use 'long words', as this can make it rather inaccessible.

Another critical approach to psychology is that of feminist psychology. This is quite difficult to define since there are many different kinds of feminism (radical, liberal, socialist, etc.) and thus many different types of feminist psychology. However, most feminists (and feminist psychologists) agree that there is inequality between men and women, and seek to address this. They differ in:

- where they see the inequality as coming from; and
- the recommendations they make for change.

CRUCIAL CONCEPT

Feminist psychology researches areas compatible with feminist concerns. Some feminist psychologists also argue that certain methods are more appropriate (qualitative, reflexive methods, see Chapter 4), since the traditional scientific method is based on 'masculine' qualities (rationality, objectivity, etc.).

Some feminist psychologists research areas of women's experience that have been neglected by mainstream psychology (e.g. menstruation, rape and lesbianism). They generally critique the sexist bias of some traditional psychology (see Chapter 4). Constructionist feminist psychologists argue that too much emphasis has been placed on gender differences in psychology, and that gender is socially constructed. However,

other feminist psychologists use traditional methods to investigate gender differences and/
or propose that men and women should be treated differently.

There was a lengthy struggle before the formation of a Psychology of Women section of
the British Psychological Society (BPS) in 1987. Opponents argued that a section would be
unnecessarily separatist and political, and that it would bring emotion into a rational
scientific discipline. Similar criticisms are still levelled at feminist psychology today.

Section summary

In this section we have covered three alternative approaches to psychology and briefly
outlined their strengths and limitations. You can probably see by now that modern
psychologists do not necessarily come from just one approach and reject all the others. It is
possible to have a cognitive physiological approach or a feminist constructionist approach,
or to be influenced by the ideas of a number of approaches. However, cognitive and
physiological approaches do still dominate mainstream psychology.

Quick test

Describe three alternative approaches to psychology, with their main assumptions and
methods.

Figure 2.6 summarises what we have covered in this chapter, including the perspective
taken by each of the approaches to the debates covered in chapter 5, so that you can relate
the two chapters together.

Approach	Psychodynamic	Behaviourist	Humanistic	Cognitive	Physiological
Main assumptions about human functioning	Based on internal, often unconscious, drives	Based on learned stimulus-response relationships (classical/operant conditioning)	Humans = unique, free individuals, innately striving to achieve full potential	Models mental processes, originally used computer model of brain, but recently a 'neural' model (connectionism)	Has biological basis in physiological processes
Methods	Case studies of therapeutic clients	Controlled experiments	Phenomenology case study of individual experience	Controlled experiments, computer/brain models	Experiments – on brain, neurons, genes, animal evolution, etc.
Scientific?	No	Yes	No – subjective	Yes	Yes
Contribution	Influenced many theorists, therapists and our 'common-sense' understanding of psychology	Improved scientific status of psychology Social learning theory Behavioural therapies	Significant impact on counselling and therapy Methods for evaluating therapy Questioned scientific method	Dominant perspective in psychology today Impact on social, developmental and clinical psychology Rigorous methods	Valuable evidence on biological bases of behaviour Psychoactive drugs to treat mental disorders
Criticisms	Untestable Subjective Lack of evidence Culturally biased	Mechanistic Limited Generalises from animals to humans	Untestable Subjective Lack of evidence Culturally biased	Artificial research Lacks integration Computer model of brain limited	Ignores environmental factors (unless interactionist)*
Determinist?	Yes (unconscious forces)	Yes (environment causes behaviour)	No (humans have free will)	No? (we reason and judge)*	Yes (biological processes)
Reductionist?	Yes – same-level explanations of behaviour sought	Yes, breaking behaviour down into S-R associations	No, autonomism – no attempt to divide humans into smaller units	Yes, machine reductionism (computer model), connectionism still reductionist.	Yes, physiological/ biological reductionism
Nature/nurture?	Both (inbuilt internal drives and impact of early childhood)	Nurture (environment)	Both (inborn motives and conditions of worth)	Both (interaction between person and environment)*	Nature (physiological processes)
Studies mental processes?	Yes – underlie all behaviour	No – only studies observable behaviour	Yes – subjective experiences of these	Yes – sees them as cognitions, like computer programs or neural networks	Yes – by direct examination of brain and neurons

* = varies between psychologists

Figure 2.6 Major approaches to psychlogy

Section 7

End of chapter assessment

Questions

These questions relate to the three assessment targets set at the beginning of this chapter. If you can answer them effectively you are in a good position to get good credit in assessments or examinations. Ideally, you should try answering each of these questions for each of the different approaches, because you should be able to describe and evaluate each one, as well as comparing each to the other approaches.

1. Describe Freud's psychodynamic approach to psychology.
2. Evaluate the humanistic approach to psychology.
3. Compare and contrast the behaviourist and cognitive approaches to psychology.

Answers

1. The word 'describe' means that this question just wants you to say what this approach is about, in other words what are its main assumptions and theories (content), and how does it study people (method)? Notice that it asks for a description of **Freud**'s psychodynamic approach. This means that you don't need to include the other psychodynamic theorists who followed Freud.

   If this was a 'short answer' question on an exam, all you have to do is to give the information contained in Figure 2.1 and in the bullet points underneath it about Freud's methods. It would be fine to use bullet points and/or tables to make it clear and concise.

   If this was an essay question, you would want to give it more of a context, and write in full paragraphs (although diagrams can be used). Have an introduction explaining that Freud was the first person to propose a psychodynamic approach to psychological matters, then go through each of the assumptions and methods of his approach, giving some examples (e.g. of defence mechanisms) to show that you understand them. Finish off with a conclusion summarising the main points and some implications of Freud's approach.

2. 'Evaluate' means 'weigh up the strengths and weaknesses'. However, you need to briefly introduce the approach, otherwise the reader won't know what you are talking about! If this is a 'short answer' exam question, you would want to briefly mention the main ideas behind the approach (seeing humans as unique, free and with an inborn motivation to achieve their full potential), before giving the main strengths and weaknesses of the approach. It might even be helpful to lay this out in a table with each of the humanist ideas followed by their strengths and weaknesses.

   If this is a coursework question, such a table might again be a good way for you to plan the essay, because it would get your ideas clear. You'd want to read up in more depth about the ideas covered in section 3 of this chapter and include the information you obtain in your essay plan. For the essay itself, remember to use a nice clear structure. You could have three subsections: a brief introduction to the approach (only a paragraph or so), its positive contributions and then its limitations. Alternatively, you could go through each of the key ideas and methods in separate sections, describing them and weighing up their strengths and weaknesses. Have a clear introduction at the start explaining how you intend to structure the essay, and a conclusion at the end summarising the contributions of the approach and why it is not a main approach in academic psychology today.

3. This is the most complex type of question you are likely to get, since it involves elements of both the first types of question, and also comparing two different approaches. The main things you have to do in such an essay are:

- describe both the approaches, stating how they are similar and different (e.g. similar methods, but different assumptions about mental processes);
- evaluate the relative strengths and weakness of the two approaches: in what ways is each better than the other? (e.g. behaviourism sticks with observable behaviour, whereas cognitive psychology models things that we can't directly observe; but behaviourism cannot explain complex behaviours, because they need some account of mental processes).

Try to use explicit examples to support what you are saying, e.g. of the type of complex behaviours that cognitive psychology has modelled. For this question, better marks would be obtained if you displayed awareness of the historical context covered in Chapter 1 (i.e. that cognitivism largely replaced behaviourism as the main approach in western psychology). Also, it would be good to show that you were 'up to date' by mentioning connectionism, perhaps relating this back to behaviourism by pointing out that it is founded on several principles of association that originated with the behaviourists.

Section 8

Further reading and research

Most introductory psychology textbooks summarise the different approaches to psychology. I found the following two particularly useful:

Eysenck, M. (2000) *Psychology: A Student's Handbook.* Hove: Psychology Press.
Malim, T. and Birch, A. (1998) *Introductory Psychology.* London: Macmillan Press.

Most of the introductory textbooks are pretty huge. For a nice summary of some of the main approaches in a little book that is easier to read in the bath, try:

Gross, R. and McIlveen, R. (1999) *Perspectives in Psychology.* London: Hodder & Stoughton.

A very full discussion of several of the main approaches in psychology and how they view human nature can be found in:

Ashworth, P. (2000) *Psychology and 'Human Nature'.* Hove: Psychology Press.

The crucial studies mentioned here can all be found in:

Banyard, P. and Grayson, A. (2000) *Introducing Psychological Research.* Basingstoke: Palgrave.

A thorough discussion of current views on Freud can be found in *The Psychologist* special issue, 'Freud in a modern light' (December, 2000).

Icon books publish helpful 'introducing' guides to 'mind and brain' and 'evolutionary psychology', for easy introductions to the ideas in the physiological approach. Their book on 'consciousness' also covers some of the more complex ideas in cognitivism (especially relating to computer models of the brain).

Few introductory texts include new-paradigm approaches, but you can find out more about feminist and constructionist approaches in Vivien Burr's books:

Burr, V. (1998) *Gender and Social Psychology.* London: Routledge.
Burr, V. (1995) *An Introduction to Social Constructionism.* London: Routledge.

Chapter 3
Pure and applied psychology

Chapter summary

At the end of Chapter 1 we saw that psychologists can study many different topics (see Figure 1.5). Most psychologists specialise and focus on one particular topic in their work. We group those who work on similar topics into sub-disciplines or fields. For example, the psychologists who study how children psychologically change as they grow up are located in the sub-discipline of developmental psychology and are therefore called developmental psychologists.

Chapter 2 introduced the idea of approaches to psychology. It is important to understand how these relate to sub-disciplines. Basically, psychologists in each sub-discipline could come from any of the approaches. For example, a developmental psychologist could take the psychodynamic approach (that children develop through Freud's stages of psycho-sexual development), the cognitive approach (that children develop through cognitive stages, displaying different mental abilities at each stage), or any of the other approaches. Some sub-disciplines in psychology are specifically linked to one approach (e.g. cognitive psychology to the cognitive approach, biological psychology to the physiological approach), but it is generally possible to study any topic (sub-discipline) from the perspective of any approach.

This chapter introduces you to some of the main sub-disciplines of psychology. These are divided into 'pure' and 'applied' psychology. The chapter also covers some issues involved in doing psychological research and applying it to people in the 'real world'.

Assessment targets

Target 1: Explaining the distinctions between pure and applied psychology
The sub-disciplines in psychology are generally divided into 'pure' psychology and 'applied' psychology. This chapter will help you to understand the difference between these, and some issues around this distinction. Question 1 at the end of the chapter tests your grasp of this.

Target 2: Describing the different types of pure and applied psychology
There are several sub-disciplines within pure psychology. This chapter will introduce you to the four main ones: biological, cognitive, developmental and social psychology. Applied psychology can also be divided into sub-disciplines such as clinical, educational, occupational and criminological/legal psychology. This chapter will outline these main branches of applied psychology. Question 2 at the end of the chapter tests your ability to describe these sub-disciplines.

Target 3: Understanding the ethical principles in psychology
Psychologists need to study humans in order to be able to understand them and explain their behaviour. However, there are many ethical problems involved in experimenting on human beings (and other animals). This chapter will help you to understand these problems, and will overview the ethical principles involved in pure and applied psychological research so that you will be able to describe these. You will also learn about some famous (or infamous) past studies that have raised ethical problems, and ethically controversial applications of psychology. Question 4 at the end of the chapter tests your understanding of these ethical issues.

How will you be assessed on this?

Throughout your psychology degree it will be important that you understand how psychology is broken down into different sub-disciplines (or topics of study). You may well be asked essay and exam questions on introductory modules about: the structure of psychology, the pure/applied distinction, the branches of psychology and the ways in which psychology has been applied in the past (controversial and non-controversial). Ethics is another major issue that is covered throughout the psychology degree. In an introductory course, you may well be asked exam questions about the ethical guidelines and what they mean. You will also have to write about ethical considerations in all of your practical research methods reports.

Section 1

Distinguishing between pure and applied psychology

In this section we will define pure and applied psychology and examine why there is a distinction between the two.

CRUCIAL CONCEPT

Pure psychology refers to psychology as an academic discipline and is also known as basic, theoretical or academic psychology. It aims to advance psychology by testing theories with observations. Pure psychologists carry out research for its own sake in order to increase knowledge and understanding about psychological matters. Pure psychology is theory-oriented.

CRUCIAL CONCEPT

Applied psychology refers to the application of psychology to professional or 'real-world' settings. Applied psychological research is usually carried out in order to investigate a practical and/or social problem. Applied psychologists are professionals with training in psychology who use psychological techniques to address such problems. Applied psychology is problem-oriented.

Pure psychology is the type of psychology often carried out by psychologists who work in universities, colleges or research institutes. Many of your lecturers are likely to be pure psychologists, carrying out research to test theories about aspects of mental processes or behaviour. There is a strong emphasis in pure psychology on publishing research papers in academic journals. Most lecturers research and publish as part of their job, since university funding depends on this as well as on teaching. Applied psychologists, on the other hand, tend to work outside of higher education in hospitals, schools, businesses, etc. They often work alongside other professionals such as psychiatrists, police officers, teachers or managers. They may be paid by a government institution (like the Home Office or the European Commission), or by an independent organisation, or they may be in private practice and be paid directly by their clients. Some of your lecturers may be applied psychologists. It is still important for them to publish papers, but they are also likely to be involved in consultancy work for organisations.

The Crucial studies below give you one example of a pure psychology study and one of an applied study to help you to appreciate the difference between them.

CRUCIAL STUDY

An example of a pure psychological study is the 'Stroop' task (Stroop, 1935): colour words are presented to participants in different colour inks. For example, the word 'blue' is presented, but it is written in red ink. There is a theory in psychology that people find it harder to process material if the format in which it is presented is incompatible with the content of the information (La Berge, 1975). Stroop task studies have found evidence to support the theory, because people are slower to name the colour of the print when the word written represents a different colour (e.g. the word 'blue' in red ink) than when it represents the same colour (e.g. the word 'blue' in blue ink).

CRUCIAL TIP

The Stroop task is an easy one to try yourself. On one bit of paper, write a list of ten colour words all in different colour inks to the words ('yellow' in green ink, 'blue' in red ink, etc.). Then, on another bit of paper, write a list of ten colour words in the same colour ink ('red' in red ink, 'blue' in blue ink etc.) Get a friend to list the colours of the ink that the words are presented in, one list at a time. Time how long they take to go through each list and compare how long they take on each.

CRUCIAL STUDY

An example of an applied psychological study is Leather and colleagues' work on pub violence. They were asked to help a brewery that had a problem with violence in some of its pubs. They analysed the 'incident report forms' that were filled out by pub staff after a violent incident (Beale et al., 1998). This enabled them to investigate how such incidents began, and how they progressed. They also analysed customer perceptions of pubs (Leather and Lawrence, 1995). Leather and colleagues found several aspects of pubs that affected expectations of violence. Customers were more likely to see violence as acceptable if the pub had an environment that made it look like violence was expected, for example having chairs and tables fixed to the floor, an untidy bar and big unfriendly doormen. Violence could be reduced by training pub staff in non-confrontational ways of dealing with aggressive customers. For example, it is not a good idea to come up behind a person in an argument and tap them on the shoulder; they are likely to hit you! Applied psychologists also developed and ran training programmes for staff in the pubs.

Why distinguish between pure and applied psychology?

Although they seem quite different on the face of it, there is actually a lot of overlap between pure and applied psychology:

- Pure theories and research are often applied to 'real-world' settings. For example, in Chapter 2 we saw how Pavlov's research on classical conditioning has led to phobia therapies like desensitisation. The Stroop task has been adapted to investigate attention bias in anxious people. When threatening and neutral words are presented in different colour inks, anxious people take longer to name ink-colour for the threatening words (Matthews and MacLeod, 1985). The results of such studies could be applied to predict which people are prone to anxiety. They may lead to the development of new therapies for anxious people (see the Crucial Study Text on cognitive psychology for more information on this 'emotional Stroop task').

- Applied psychology often yields theories and techniques for pure psychology. For example, psychoanalytic theories developed out of Freud's clinical work with clients; intelligence tests developed in an applied setting when the French government wanted to identify children with learning difficulties and give them remedial education. Research on the causes of pub violence is likely to feed back into 'pure' theories of aggression.

- Many psychologists work across pure and applied psychology. Malim and Birch (1998) give the example of the Cognition and Brain Sciences Unit at Cambridge

61

University. Research there has addressed practical problems (e.g. the effective design of decimal coinage) and theoretical issues (e.g. the function of attention and memory).

Howitt (1991) states that it was partly psychologists' desire to be seen as scientists that led to this pure/applied distinction (see Chapter 4). Psychology has been modelled on other sciences which seemed to be broken down in this way. The distinction depicts pure psychology as the 'real' psychology and superior to applied psychology, which is merely the offspring of psychology (Gale, 1994). Both pure and applied psychologists have objected to this distinction. It undermines the highly demanding, rigorous nature of applied psychology. It also suggests that pure psychology cannot be performed in, or applied to, real-world settings. This may result in pure psychology being inadequately funded. This distinction in psychology causes an artificial split between pure 'scientists' and applied 'practitioners'. It is important that there is communication between pure and applied psychologists for pure psychology to be useful and meaningful to the real world and for applied psychology to be rigorous and to advance psychology in general.

Why have applied psychology?

Some people have argued that applied psychology is entirely unnecessary, pointing out that people were managing organisations, teaching, making laws, advertising and helping others for a long time before psychology emerged as a discipline. A joke about applied psychologists is that they tell you what you already know in words that you don't understand! So another important question is what applied psychology can give that experience and common-sense cannot (see section 4 of Chapter 5 for more about common sense and psychology). Here are a few answers that have been put forward to this question (Coolican et al., 1996):

- **Use of the scientific method.** Applied psychologists are trained in rigorous techniques for investigating issues, whereas someone without training may easily jump to the wrong conclusion or think they have found a simple solution. For example, imagine that a local education authority found that there was a much bigger problem with bullying in some of its schools than others. The schools with high levels of bullying were older and larger than the other ones. Somebody untrained in scientific methods might jump to a conclusion based on the obvious differences and/or their own preconceptions, deciding that the only solution is newer, smaller schools. An applied psychologist, on the other hand, would have the methods to find out whether it is age or size of school which impacts on levels of bullying, or whether it is another related or unrelated factor. For example, older schools may be more traditional in structure, leading to a culture more accepting of bullying between both staff and pupils. Larger schools might have worse playground environments, with more hidden areas where bullying can take place. These issues could be addressed without the need for whole new schools. (See Chapter 4 for details about how the scientific method works, and Boulton's chapter in Hartley and Branthwaite (1999) for more on how psychology has been applied to bullying.)

- **Drawing on psychological knowledge and theories.** Applied psychologists should be able to evaluate theories and research findings in order to determine their strengths and limitations, and to decide whether they can be usefully applied to an area. For example, there are many different theories about how to change behaviour. An applied psychologist asked to design an anti-smoking campaign can read up on these and determine which can be usefully applied. They can also evaluate past research on anti-smoking campaigns and similar health promotions to see what has worked well in the past (Banyard, 1996).

- **Membership of a professional group.** The BPS can validate applied psychologists who have sound psychological training, giving them chartered status. It can also strike off anybody who is found to be incompetent or unprofessional. This way people can ensure that the applied psychologist they hire is thoroughly trained and professional. Chartered psychologists also have to follow the BPS ethical guidelines (see section 4).

- **Interventions and evaluations.** Applied psychologists are trained to know how to construct interventions and put them into place (such as an anti-bullying or anti-smoking campaign in schools), and how to evaluate whether they are effective. It is important that interventions follow a cycle like that shown in Figure 3.1.

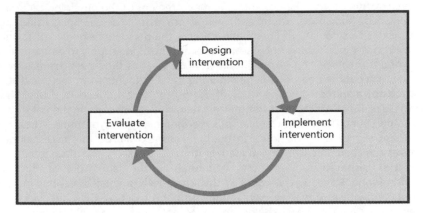

Figure 3.1 The intervention cycle

Section summary

In this section we have outlined what is meant by pure and applied psychology, and also seen that this distinction is somewhat artificial. However, the sub-disciplines in psychology are usually broken down into pure and applied areas, and this is how sections 2 and 3 of this chapter will be structured. Finally, in this section, we have seen what is gained from having applied psychology.

Quick test

What are pure and applied psychology? Is it useful to distinguish the two?

Section 2

Branches of pure psychology

This section briefly outlines the different branches of pure psychology, giving a crucial study to illustrate each one. These sub-disciplines are divided up in different ways in different courses and textbooks. Here I focus on biological, cognitive, developmental and social psychology. Other texts may also include the following as separate sub-disciplines: comparative psychology and learning (which are mentioned as part of biological psychology here), individual differences and abnormal psychology (which are mentioned in section 4 of this chapter, and covered in depth in the Crucial Study Text on individual differences).

────────CRUCIAL TIP────────

Go to the BPS web site to see how they divide psychology up into sections (areas of scientific knowledge): www.bps.org.uk.

Biological psychology

Biological psychology is also known as biopsychology or psychobiology. It is the sub-division that is interested in the biological basis of behaviour. The psychobiology section of the BPS includes the following areas:

- **Physiological psychology.** The overall study of the influence on human psychology of bodily processes, such as brain functioning and hormonal levels.
- **Psychophysiology.** The non-intrusive measurement of the physiological processes involved in human behaviour and mental processes. For example, using surface electrodes to stimulate the brain and observe the person's response, or taking PET (positron emission tomography) scans to record the blood supply to different areas of the brain when a person carries out different tasks. (This shows which areas are most active, since those neurons will be requiring most nutrients from the blood supply.)
- **Psychopharmacology.** The study of the psychological effects of drugs. This can give clues about which neurotransmitter chemicals are involved in mental states. For example, amphetamines can cause schizophrenic-type symptoms. These drugs increase the levels of dopamine in the brain, so it could be that excess dopamine causes schizophrenia (the dopamine hypothesis – see section 2 of Chapter 5).
- **Animal behaviour.** The study of animals in the laboratory or the natural environment. Some psychologists in this area study animal behaviour in its own right, and others use it to gain insight into the mechanisms underlying human behaviour. Comparative psychology makes comparisons between different species of animal, and between animals and humans.
- **Behavioural genetics.** The study of the influence of genes on behaviour – see section 3 of Chapter 5.
- **Learning theory.** The theory of how learning occurs, including the conditioning theories covered in Chapter 2 and Köhler's 'insight learning' covered in Chapter 1.
- **Neuropsychology.** The study of the brain processes involved in human psychology. This often involves examining the abilities of brain-damaged patients to draw inferences about the function of brain areas.

CRUCIAL STUDY

Dement and Kleitman (1957) studied the physiological processes underlying dreaming. They brought participants into a sleep laboratory and recorded changes in eye movement and brainwaves over the course of the night, waking participants up at various intervals to ask them if they were dreaming. There was a high incidence of dream recall in Rapid Eye Movement (REM) periods, and a very low incidence at other times. Eye movements during REM sleep reflected the content of the dream. For example, people showing pure vertical eye movements, when awakened, reported dreams of climbing ladders or cliffs, or throwing basketballs into a net. People who showed little eye movement for a few minutes reported staring fixedly at something in their dream. The eye movements were remarkably comparable to those occurring during similar real-life activities.

Related research has found that there is a REM rebound if people are deprived of REM sleep: they compensate by having a greater proportion of REM sleep the following night. Psychologists are still not sure of the function of dreams. They may simply provide stimulation while asleep, they may aid the developing brain (since babies have much more REM sleep than adults), or they might serve some cognitive function: consolidating memory, aiding learning or problem solving, or dealing with emotional arousal (see Horne, 2001).

CRUCIAL TIP

Relate this to section 5 of Chapter 2 on the physiological approach to psychology and section 3 of Chapter 5 on the nature-nurture debate.

Cognitive psychology

Cognitive psychology is the sub-discipline of psychology that deals with cognitions (mental processes). It tends to focus on the 'higher-order' processes (those involved in memory or decision-making, rather than breathing or walking). Here are some of the main areas studied:

- **Perception.** This is the way that we make sense of information picked up by our senses (sights, sounds, tastes, etc.) Figure 1.4 displays some of the illusions used by Gestalt psychologists to study visual perception. An example of a study in perception is Kozlowski and Cutting's (1977) research, which found that people can recognise the sex of a person just from seeing the movement of points of light attached to their joints (shoulders, elbows, wrists, hips, knees and ankles).

- **Attention.** This is the way we focus our awareness on things so that we're prepared to respond to them, for example on the other person in a conversation. One classic study in this area is Cherry's (1953) research on the 'cocktail party effect'. This refers to the common experience of people at parties that they are able to focus on their own conversation despite all the conversations going on in the room, but that they are also able to shift attention instantly if someone in another conversation mentions their name. Cherry found that we can selectively attend to one conversation if the others going on are physically different (further away, or in a different pitch or intensity of voice). If two messages are presented in the same voice to both ears at once it is very hard to follow one and ignore the other, just on the basis of meaning. By the way, Cherry's name is very easy to remember in relation to this study – what do we have in our drinks at a cocktail party?

- **Language.** This is how we communicate with each other by organising words into meaningful combinations. Cognitive psychologists study words, the way they are combined (syntax) and their meanings (semantics). Section 3 of Chapter 5 covers theories of language acquisition. Chomsky is a major theorist within the cognitive psychology of language.

- **Problem-solving.** This is the way we find solutions to problems. Cognitive psychologists often study how people and computers solve puzzles like the tower of Hanoi (Newell and Simon, 1972) or the hobbits and orcs problem (Thomas, 1974). (See Figure 3.2 – try to solve the problems before reading on.)

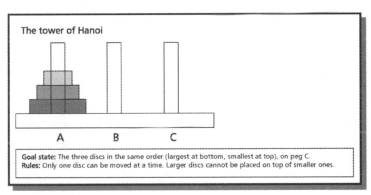

The tower of Hanoi

A B C

Goal state: The three discs in the same order (largest at bottom, smallest at top), on peg C.
Rules: Only one disc can be moved at a time. Larger discs cannot be placed on top of smaller ones.

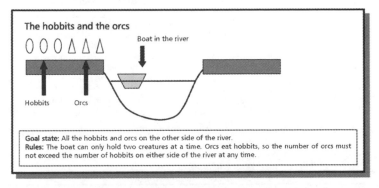

The hobbits and the orcs

Boat in the river

Hobbits Orcs

Goal state: All the hobbits and orcs on the other side of the river.
Rules: The boat can only hold two creatures at a time. Orcs eat hobbits, so the number of orcs must not exceed the number of hobbits on either side of the river at any time.

Figure 3.2 Problems used in problem-solving research

Computer models have helped to explain how people solve such problems, for example we use means–ends analysis, finding the difference between our current state in the problem and the goal state, and producing a sub-goal that will decrease this difference: in the tower of Hanoi, if there is a choice between putting the largest disc on the middle peg or the end peg, we will put it on the end peg. The hobbits and orcs problem is difficult because one move is inconsistent with means-ends analysis (a hobbit and an orc must return to the starting point). However, such findings do not help to explain how we solve the ill-defined problems of everyday life (like writing an essay or organising a party). Also, computer programs have different difficulties with such problems to human problem-solvers. This is a snag for the computer-mind analogy of the early cognitivist approach but not for the more recent 'connectionist' approach that uses a 'neural' model of the brain (see Chapter 2).

- **Memory.** This is the storage and retrieval of information. There are many different psychological theories of how memory works. For example, the 'two-process' theory argues that information comes into short-term memory and is easily forgotten unless it is rehearsed and goes into the long-term memory. The 'levels of processing' theory argues that how we process information determines how well it is retained. Shallow processing relates to physical characteristics (e.g. whether a word is written in upper or lower case). Deep processing relates to meaning (e.g. what a word actually means) (Craik and Lockhart, 1972). This explains why we remember things more accurately and for longer if we understand them than if we have just learned them by 'rote'.

CRUCIAL STUDY

One well-known memory study is Loftus and Palmer's (1974) research into the validity of eyewitness testimony. They showed participants film-clips of traffic accidents, and asked questions afterwards, using differing wording. They found that memories were distorted by the 'leading questions' used. If participants were asked how fast the cars were going when they 'smashed into' each other they would give a higher speed than if they were asked how fast they were going when they 'hit' each other. When they were asked the former question they were also more likely to respond positively to the additional question 'did you see any broken glass', even though there was no broken glass in the film.

CRUCIAL TIP

Relate this to section 4 of Chapter 2 on the cognitive approach to psychology. There is also a Crucial Study Text focusing specifically on cognitive psychology.

Developmental psychology

Developmental psychology studies how people change and develop, particularly in relation to their social and cognitive abilities and behaviour. In the past, developmental psychology

Stage	Age	Characteristics
Sensorimotor	0–2	• Children learn the basic rules of space, time and causality, but are not aware of the rules they are using. • They learn to differentiate themselves from the rest of the world. • They develop object permanence (realising that objects continue to exist even when out of sight).
Preoperational	2–7	• Children become able to represent things with images and language. • They are egocentric (can only see the world from their viewpoint and can't imagine how someone else would see it). • They can't conserve (e.g. they can't understand that if you spread out some buttons there are still the same number as there were to begin with, that if you change the shape of a ball of Plasticine it keeps the same mass, or that if you pour liquid from a fat beaker into a thin one, there is still the same amount of liquid – see figure 3.4). • They can't reverse mental operations (if they've seen an action occur they can't mentally 'rewind the tape').
Concrete operations	7–11	• Children gradually learn how to conserve and reverse and are no longer egocentric. • They are able to think logically, but need to experiment with real objects in order to solve problems.
Formal operations	11 onwards	• Children can reason abstractly.

Figure 3.3 Piaget's developmental stages

focused on childhood and adolescence, but in the last thirty years adulthood and old age have also been regarded as developmental stages (the lifespan approach). One of the key theorists in developmental psychology is Piaget. His developmental stages are shown in Figure 3.3.

CRUCIAL STUDY

Samuel and Bryant (1984) re-examined some of the experiments that Piaget used to come up with his developmental stages. They focused on the conservation tasks shown in Figure 3.4. In the conservation of mass experiment an adult would show a child two lumps of plasticine the same size. She would ask 'which one is bigger?' and the child would say 'they're both the same'. She would then roll one of the lumps into a sausage and ask the same question. The preoperational child would answer 'the sausage is bigger', while the child who has the ability to conserve mass (reached at around age seven) would still say they were both the same. The preoperational child can't reverse the adult's actions (rewind the tape recorder) to realise that both lumps are still the same size, so they intuitively answer that the sausage-shaped one looks bigger. Similarly, in the conservation of number and volume studies, preoperational children said that there were more buttons in one row than the other after the buttons were spread out, and that there was more liquid in one beaker than the other after the liquid in one beaker was poured into a long, thin beaker.

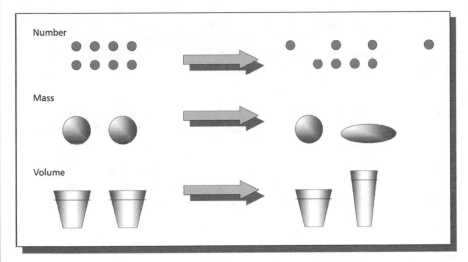

Figure 3.4 Piaget's conservation tasks

Samuel and Bryant proposed that the results of these studies might not be due to the cognitive limitations of the children, but to the structure of the tasks and demand characteristics (Orne – 1962, see section 3 of Chapter 4). Children in the studies were always asked the same question twice: once before the adult had made a change and once afterwards. In real life, most of the time when a child is asked a question twice it is because they got the answer wrong the first time, so repeating the question might lead them to think that their first answer was wrong and change it. Samuel and Bryant found that if you just asked the question once, after the change, children made fewer errors. This does not invalidate Piaget's stages, as children still grasped conservation between 5 and 8 years of age, but it does display the importance of being very careful about research procedures.

CRUCIAL TIP

There is a discussion of Erikson and Kohlberg's theories in Chapter 4, Freud's theories in section 1 of Chapter 2, and Bandura's study in section 3 of Chapter 2. These are all key ideas in developmental psychology. There is also a Crucial Study Text focusing specifically on developmental psychology.

Social psychology

Social psychology is the sub-discipline of psychology that is concerned with social behaviour, such as how we form relationships and groups, anti-social and pro-social behaviour (aggression and helping), and how we use verbal and non-verbal communication in conversations. It is also concerned with the ways in which our thoughts, feelings and behaviours are influenced by other people. For example, Asch (1955) found that a person in a group will often give an obviously incorrect answer to a question if everyone else in the group has given that answer before them. Other psychologists have found that people act differently in a crowd than they would as an individual, being less likely to help others and more likely to display aggression (Festinger, Pepitone and Newcombe, 1952). There are many examples of traditional social psychology scattered throughout the rest of this book, particularly in section 4 of this chapter (which contains Milgram's obedience study and Zimbardo's prison simulation), and in Chapter 4 (research on the impact of media violence, Pennebaker's work on expressing emotions, and the studies on the impact of the research experiment situation).

The dominant approach in social psychology in recent years has been social cognition, which was introduced in section 4 of Chapter 2. This suggests that we have cognitive scripts, which help us know how to behave in different social situations, and prototypes of people based on the group they are from (for example, imagine a prototypical student, lecturer or builder). An alternative perspective to traditional social psychology is social constructionism (see section 6 of Chapter 2). Potter and Edwards' discourse analysis studies are examples of social constructionist research.

--- CRUCIAL STUDY ---

Potter and Edwards' (1990) paper analyses a dispute between the politician Nigel Lawson and some journalists about what Lawson said in a meeting. It shows how both sides of the dispute used language to make their point of view sound like 'fact'. The journalists made their side sound convincing by questioning how all of them could have misunderstood what Lawson said. Lawson argued that the journalists had not reached 'consensus' but had 'colluded' and created the story after the meeting, otherwise their versions of events would not have matched so exactly. Both sides used the detail that ten journalists were in agreement to support their argument. They used argumentative techniques to persuade others that their story was the one to believe.

Section summary

In this section I have briefly introduced the sub-disciplines of pure psychology and given an overview of the areas they cover. The example studies here should help you to understand clearly the kind of research carried out in each area, and I have also mentioned relevant sections of the rest of the book that you can refer to for more examples or to get a deeper understanding of the issues in each sub-discipline. You should also tie this section in with what you learn in section 4 about the ethical issues involved in researching psychology.

Quick test

Briefly describe what biological, cognitive, developmental and social psychology are, giving one example of a study in each.

Section 3

Branches of applied psychology

This section covers applied psychology, outlining four of the main applied sub-disciplines of applied psychology: clinical, educational, occupational and criminological/legal psychology.

These are the main areas of professional psychology that someone could work in following a psychology degree, other than psychology teaching or pure research (see BPS website).

In order to become a chartered applied psychologist in one of these professional areas at least a 2:1 in a BPS-recognised undergraduate degree is usually required, plus some postgraduate training. This usually has to be funded by the student themselves, except in the case of clinical psychology, although there are sometimes grants and bursaries that can be applied for. Once a person has the relevant training and experience they can apply to the BPS to be put on the Register of Chartered Psychologists.

In this section the kind of work done by each type of applied psychologist is outlined along with the training required. Some other related branches of applied psychology are also mentioned along the way.

CRUCIAL TIP

Go to the BPS website to see how they divide psychology up into divisions (professional areas): www.bps.org.uk. The BPS also provides information about opportunities and careers in psychology, which you can obtain by e-mailing, phoning or writing to them.

Clinical psychology

We came across clinical psychology in Chapter 1 when we looked at what psychology is and isn't. Clinical psychology is the branch of psychology that is most often confused with psychiatry and counselling, because clinical psychologists also work with people with physical and mental health problems and use many of the same therapies. However, clinical psychologists are trained in psychology rather than in medicine (and are therefore not able to prescribe drugs like a psychiatrist).

After their degree, a person who wants to become a clinical psychologist has to get some experience in the area (often by working as an assistant psychologist in a clinical setting). After that they can apply for a masters course in clinical psychology, which usually lasts for three years. The NHS pays trainee clinical psychologists a salary during their course, and they gain experience of working with various groups (e.g. adults, children, the elderly, people with learning difficulties) as well as being assessed on assignments and attending lectures and seminars. It is hard for mature students over 35 to get funding for clinical training because they won't be able to work for so long after they qualify.

Clinical psychologists apply psychology to health care, diagnosing psychological problems such as depression, schizophrenia, Alzheimer's disease or eating disorders and then using therapies to try to alleviate them. They also work with people with physical problems related to psychological health, for example helping someone adjust to having a disability, or providing stress management training to someone with high blood pressure. Most clinical psychologists work directly with individual patients, families or groups in a health service or private setting, often a hospital or a community health practice. They generally work in a team alongside medical professionals (doctors, nurses, physiotherapists, etc.). Clinical psychologists are trained in various different therapies. Some use a mixture of different therapies and others specialise more. The main types of therapy are the psychodynamic, humanist, behavioural and cognitive therapies (all of which were introduced in Chapter 2).

Here is a clinical psychology case study to illustrate the type of work involved:

> Ann lived in London, but found it very difficult to commute to work because she had a fear of enclosed spaces, and this made travelling on the tube almost impossible. Whenever she tried she panicked, her heart raced and she was scared she was going to faint and that everyone would stare at her. Her GP referred her to a clinical psychologist who used a combination of behavioural and cognitive therapies with her. On the

cognitive side, he challenged some of her unrealistic fears about her panics. He told her that panicked people are unlikely to faint because they are in the wrong bodily state to do so, and he challenged the idea that everyone would stare by taking her out into the street, acting oddly and getting her to observe other people's reactions. Most people just ignored him! On the behavioural side, he used desensitisation therapy over several weeks, gradually getting her to relax in a tube station, then walking down the stairs, then in the train, and then on a short tube journey.

A related sub-discipline of psychology is counselling psychology. Counselling psychologists also use therapies to help clients and may work privately, for an organisation or for the health service. Following their degree, counselling psychologists do a two- or three-year BPS-recognised masters or diploma, which usually has to be self-funded. Counselling psychology may be a good alternative to clinical psychology for students over 35 who want to work with people with psychological problems.

CRUCIAL TIP

If you think you'd like to be a clinical or counselling psychologist, it might well be helpful to get some experience as a voluntary counsellor to see whether you enjoy that type of work. Organisations like Childline and Relate provide basic counselling training and then take people on as volunteer phone or face-to-face counsellors. There are also local organisations for people with physical disabilities, learning difficulties, chronic illnesses or psychological problems, such as befriending organisations, and many special schools and hospitals take on voluntary help. Your lecturers may have contacts with such organisations, so it is worth asking.

Other health-related areas in applied psychology are health psychology and sports psychology. Practitioners in these areas apply psychology to health, exercise and sport. They obtain a postgraduate qualification (diploma, masters or PhD), and then generally work for an organisation or in the community. For example, a health psychologist might be involved in putting together a government campaign to get people to exercise more, or they might work for an organisation, ascertaining the levels of stress among employees and putting together a stress management programme to address this (see Banyard, 1996). A sports psychologist might work with a football team, trying to improve teamwork, motivation and concentration of the players, or they might train gymnastic coaches in how to get the best performance out of child gymnasts (see Woods, 1998).

Educational psychology

Educational psychologists work with children and adolescents. They are mostly employed by local education authorities, and often work in schools, but also in other settings such as the home, special units, guidance clinics and social services. Educational psychologists have to have teaching experience, so many of them do a postgraduate certificate in education following their psychology degree, teach for at least two years, and then do postgraduate training in educational psychology. After this, they are supervised closely for the first year of their post. Some educational psychologists start off as teachers, and then take a psychology degree and an educational psychology postgraduate course.

Educational psychologists apply psychology to all kinds of issues:

- **physical problems** – helping children with physical or neurological impairment, for example ensuring that children with hearing problems understand lessons and fit in with the other children, making sure the curriculum content is appropriate for them;

- **educational problems** – working with children with learning difficulties or special needs, for example diagnosing children with dyslexia and giving them appropriate support, or providing additional help for particularly gifted children;

- **behavioural problems** – dealing with children who are disruptive, aggressive or delinquent, for example, helping a school to bring in an anti-bullying policy, or following up a child who consistently truants from school to find out what is going on;

- **emotional problems** – supporting children who have depression, anxiety, school phobia or poor relationships with their peers, for example bringing in group counselling for children whose classmate has died in a car crash, or working in a guidance clinic for pregnant teenagers to help them to adjust emotionally

As you can see, educational psychologists are involved in assessing children to determine whether there is a problem and what it is (by observing the child, interviewing them and those around them, and/or giving them psychological tests). After assessment, the educational psychologist may work with the child, or bring in some kind of intervention via the school or family. Alternatively they might refer a child to somebody else, for example a clinical psychologist, speech therapist, doctor or social worker.

Occupational psychology

Occupational/industrial psychologists apply psychology to the workplace in many different ways and are mostly employed by organisations. Their aim is generally to increase the effectiveness of the organisation and the job satisfaction of the employees. Psychologists can go straight into organisations following their undergraduate degree, to work in selection, training, job design, etc. However, to become a chartered occupational psychologist you need a postgraduate course in occupational, organisational or industrial psychology (these come under many different names since occupational psychology covers several different areas). Here are just a few of them:

- **Organisational consultancy.** This involves areas like the management of organisational change and development, for example helping the workforce adjust when an organisation grows, diversifies into another area or starts using a new technology. Consultant occupational psychologists can help the organisation to adapt its structure to one that is more effective; they can train people in leadership, assertiveness and other communication skills. They can be involved in industrial relations negotiations between employees, management and trade unions. They can also work with those who are retiring or being made redundant.

- **Personnel management.** Another big area in occupational psychology is selection and training. Psychologists can be involved in assessing the need for recruitment and developing a selection procedure using appropriate interviews, psychometric tests, work samples, etc. They may be involved in putting equal opportunities policies and harassment procedures in place. They may also be brought in to assess training needs and develop programmes to appraise and evaluate staff, and to provide career guidance.

- **Ergonomics.** Occupational psychologists in this area focus on the interaction between people and their work environment, investigating whether the environment is suitable for the job. For example, ergonomic psychologists work on the design of chairs, desks and computers along with engineers and physiologists to ensure that people don't strain their eyes or put themselves at risk of repetitive strain injury (RSI).

- **Organisational health.** This type of occupational psychology involves assessing the health and safety of employees and bringing in interventions to improve matters. The pub violence research mentioned in section 1 is organisational health psychology, since it involves assessing the risk of injury to pub staff and designing interventions to decrease the risk (e.g. staff training and altering the work environment). Psychologists in this area might also be involved in assessing the risk of accidents in people doing shift work, or putting stress management programmes in place. Work-related stress is a particularly important area in occupational psychology today since organisations have been taken to court for failing to help employees suffering from stress.

Hayward's (1996) book is a good overview of this area of applied psychology.

Criminological and legal psychology

Of all the branches of applied psychology, this is the one that attracts the most attention, and the most confusion (see Chapter 1). TV programmes and films like *Cracker* and *Copycat* depict criminal psychology in a way that is both narrow (focusing on offender profiling of serial killers) and unrealistic (the criminal psychologists seem to have almost supernatural abilities and get personally involved in and endangered by cases). Psychologists can actually work in all parts of the criminal and legal system, in courts and prisons as well as with the police. Offender profiling is only a very tiny branch of this type of psychology.

Following their psychology degree, psychologists in this area have to do a masters degree in criminological psychology, investigative psychology or forensic psychology. To get on to one of these courses they often have to have relevant work experience. Another route into criminal psychology is to train as a clinical psychologist and then specialise in forensic psychology, or to do a PhD in an area of criminal psychology.

Here are some of the different areas of criminological/legal psychology:

- **Forensic psychology.** This generally happens after an arrest is made, and includes the following areas:

  - **legal psychology in court** – psychologists may be expert witnesses assessing whether a criminal is mentally ill, or may be involved in trial strategy, juror selection, helping children to be witnesses, or in evaluating how valid eyewitness testimonies are (see section 2 of this chapter and section 1 of Chapter 5);
  - **clinical psychology in prisons/hospitals** – psychologists evaluate prisoners, assess their needs and likelihood of reoffending, give them therapy and treatment, or are involved in other ways in rehabilitation and probation;

- **Investigative psychology.** This generally happens before an arrest is made, and includes the following areas:

  - **information retrieval** – psychologists help police to interview suspects, victims and witnesses, for example eliciting truthful, relevant and full information, calming vulnerable interviewees like children, aiding the memory of witnesses, assessing the value of hypnosis as a technique;
  - **decision-making** – psychologists may also help in the police decision-making process. Police investigating a crime are often under a lot of pressure from the public, the media, those of higher rank and the victims. Under these circumstances it is easy to make mistakes or miss vital steps in the decision-making process. Psychologists can help in this process, and also be involved in the design of computer systems, which are invaluable in linking crimes and aiding decision-making;
  - **offender profiling** – psychologists may be involved in assessing why criminals behave in the way they do and building up profiles of different types of criminal from past crimes. For example, the FBI interviewed serial murderers and came up with the categorisation of 'organised' and 'disorganised' killers. Psychologists may also be involved in profiling current criminals from crime scenes and witness accounts in order to help police catch them. This is often less about profiling personalities (like in the movies) and more about figuring out what kind of job a criminal has, or where they are likely to live. For example, when David Canter profiled the 'railway rapist', John Duffy, he deduced that the rapist lived in a certain area, based on where the crimes were committed and that he held a semi-skilled job (he was a carpenter for British Rail) (Harrower, 1998).

A lot of this branch of psychology is also about more general research into crime and criminals: understanding why crimes occur, how much crime there is, and how it can be prevented. For example, psychologists have researched the public perception of crime and found that women and the elderly fear crime most, when it is actually young men who are the most common victims (Harrower, 1998). Criminological/legal psychologists can also be involved in policy-making, offering advice on the treatment of offenders and victims.

Harrower's (1998) book is an excellent introduction to criminological/legal psychology. If you are still just fascinated by offender profiling, check out the books by criminal psychologists David Canter (*Criminal Shadows,* 1994) and Paul Britton (*The Jigsaw Man*, 1997).

There is some overlap between the different sub-disciplines of applied psychology, for example organisational health psychologists apply health psychology to occupational groups, forensic psychologists use clinical techniques with prisoners, and a child or adolescent with mental health problems might be referred to a clinical psychologist, a counselling psychologist or an educational psychologist. Applied psychologists may also carry out research and teach, like pure psychologists.

Demand for applied psychologists is increasing beyond the availability of people to meet them (Lindsay and Lunt, 1993). However, the training is long and expensive in many cases, and can be difficult to find and to get a place on.

CRUCIAL TIP

Most psychology students don't go into professional psychology. A psychology degree is a good background for employment in other jobs, particularly those requiring problem-solving abilities, statistical knowledge, computer expertise and/or communication and counselling skills. For example, many psychology students go on to careers in social work, counselling, school teaching, the police, market research, advertising, personnel, management, and information technology.

Section summary

In this section I have briefly introduced the sub-disciplines of applied psychology, the training that is needed to get into these areas and the types of work involved. You should tie this in with what you learn towards the end of section 4 about the ethical issues involved in applying psychology to people in the 'real world'.

Quick test

Briefly describe what clinical, educational, occupational and criminological/legal psychology are, giving a made-up case study for each one (like the one that I have given for clinical psychology).

Section 4

Ethics in pure and applied psychology

In this section we look at some ethical problems facing psychologists and the guidelines that have been put forward to deal with them. Psychologists have to consider ethics when doing research on humans and animals, and when applying psychology professionally.

CRUCIAL CONCEPT

Ethics in psychological research refers to the moral responsibility of the researcher to protect their participants from physical or psychological harm.

Ethical issues in psychological research

When I teach ethics to students, I always start off by considering something that most of us are familiar with today: reality TV. If you've watched programmes like *Big Brother*, have a think about the ethical issues involved in an 'experiment' like that. Do you think it is OK to put people in a situation like the 'Big Brother' house? In what ways is it ethical or not?

In thinking about this example you might have considered whether the people who volunteered to be on the show 'knew what they were getting themselves into' (**informed consent**). You may question whether people could really understand the effect that being shut in a house with complete strangers for several weeks would have on them. You could have remembered that the 'Big Brother' contestants could leave any time they wanted to (**withdrawal from the investigation**). But you may wonder whether it would be that easy to walk out of the house with the whole country watching you, knowing that you were giving up the chance of winning thousands of pounds. You might also have read that the contestants could ask to see a counsellor at any time they wanted, and that they received counselling at the end of the series (**debriefing**). Finally, you might have considered whether you would like to go on the show yourself. If you definitely would not, that probably has something to do with everyone in the TV audience being able to watch your every move. You might feel happier doing something like that if nobody would know who you were (**confidentiality and anonymity**).

Congratulations! You have just come up with most of the ethical principles that psychologists have to consider when carrying out their research.

Let's look at a famous psychological experiment that is often used to demonstrate the importance of ethics and to initiate debate over whether psychologists have the right to risk causing harm to their participants. Again, jot down any ethical problems you can see here. Try to imagine that you were a participant in the study.

CRUCIAL STUDY

In Milgram's (1963) study, people were recruited using newspaper adverts asking for participants for a study on memory. When they came to the experimental laboratory, they were told that they would be taking part in research on the effects of punishment on learning. They were shown another participant in the role of the 'learner', sitting in an isolated cubicle, wired up to a machine that could give him electric shocks. Back in the main room, our participant, the 'teacher', could not see the 'learner', but could hear him. The teacher had to ask the learner questions and give him a shock each time he got the answer wrong. Each time, they had to increase the shock by 15 volts. Milgram wasn't really interested in learning. He wanted to see how obedient the participants were. What shock level would they be prepared to go up to if the experimenter, an authority figure, kept telling them to continue the experiment?

Despite hearing screams from the learner, Milgram found that all of the participants would go up to 300 volts, and 62.5 per cent went up to the potentially lethal 450 volts. After the experiment it was revealed to the participant that the 'learner' was actually an actor. They hadn't really electrocuted him! The study demonstrates what extreme behaviour people will carry out because they are being 'obedient to authority'.

Evaluation

The ethical problems you might see with this are **protection of participants**: the research caused considerable stress and emotional conflict to those giving the 'electric shocks'. You're probably asking yourself whether the fascinating findings are worth the level of psychological harm caused; they do seem to shed light on how ordinary people come to do terrible things. The study also suggests that we should consider **deception**. Milgram had to mislead his participants. Participants would have acted differently if they had known the real nature of the study. Again, is it fair to lie to participants for the sake of interesting research? Finally, the study highlights the importance of psychologists considering all the possible outcomes of a study. Milgram did not expect that the participants would go anywhere near as far as they did. Zimbardo carried out another famous study, the prison simulation (Haney, Banks and Zimbardo, 1973). He got students to role-play being prisoners and prison guards in a fake prison. The 'guards' quickly started mistreating the 'prisoners', leading to them experiencing high levels of distress. Unlike Milgram, Zimbardo abandoned his study after six days because of the levels of distress caused. Milgram has justified not stopping his study because when he debriefed his participants afterwards, they were all glad to have taken part, and felt that they had found out something interesting about themselves.

Without human participants, there would be no psychology, because we would not be able to study human behaviour. As well as our moral responsibility to protect the rights and dignity of our participants, we need to consider ethics because people will not take part in our studies if we treat them badly. We now call these people 'participants' rather than 'subjects' because 'subject' implies a passive person who is experimented on by a more knowledgeable 'experimenter'. The word 'participant' recognises that people take part in our studies as a favour to us.

Here is a brief outline of the BPS guidelines. As you will see, they cover all the issues we have come up with so far. For a more detailed description of these issues and how they may impact on your own research as a psychology student, see the Crucial Study Text on research methods and statistics.

BPS ethical guidelines (from www.bps.org.uk, most recently updated January 2000):

- **Informed consent.** Participants should give their consent to take part in the research, fully understanding its nature and purpose. The only cases when this does not apply is when deception is necessary (see below) and when people are being observed in a public place without their knowledge. You don't need consent in this situation because people would expect strangers to be able to observe them.
- **Deception.** This should be avoided unless it is essential to the study. If so, participants should be informed as soon as possible about the real nature of the research. The BPS says that 'participants should never be deliberately misled without extremely strong scientific or medical justification'.
- **Debriefing.** This takes place when the study is over. It ensures that participants fully understand what it was about, and also checks that they are feeling OK. Participants should leave a study in at least as good a state of mind as they had when they came in. Counselling should be provided if participants are emotionally disturbed by the research in any way. This should be put in place before carrying out the research.
- **Withdrawal from the investigation.** Participants have the right to withdraw at any stage, even refusing to have their data used once they have finished taking part. They should not feel coerced into volunteering, and should understand their right to withdraw from the start. It may be hard for someone to withdraw in front of other people or if they are being paid to take part, so these things need to be considered.
- **Confidentiality and anonymity.** Confidentiality should always be maintained. This means that participants' identities will only be known to the specified researchers and not beyond this group. Anonymity is possible in some studies, like questionnaires. This is where even the researchers don't know the identity of the participants.
- **Protection of participants.** Any physical or psychological harm to participants should be avoided, including embarrassment, humiliation and damage to self-esteem.

— CRUCIAL TIP —
Make sure that you know this list. It is often asked for in exam questions.

Ethical issues in animal research

The BPS also has guidelines for the use of animals in research. Psychologists sometimes carry out research on animals, and the need to do this is hotly debated by psychologists and people in general who are concerned about animal rights. Such studies are carried out because there are seen to be sufficient similarities between animals and humans to generalise findings about, say, the visual system of a cat or the leaning behaviour of a pigeon to humans. Often it is argued that similar research on humans would not be practical or ethical. For example, it is easier to study the effects of interbreeding in rats because they reproduce much faster than humans and we can control who they mate with. However, these arguments can create the 'animal research paradox'. If animals are similar enough to compare to humans, then they may be similar enough to suffer too.

Several studies that were carried out in the past are no longer seen as ethical, for example the 'executive monkey' experiment, which studied the impact of stress on monkeys by giving them electric shocks. The monkeys who had no control over the shocks developed stomach ulcers and died. The BPS guidelines now state that we should avoid, or at least minimise, discomfort to animals and seek as much advice as possible about whether the likely scientific contribution justifies the use of living animals (Lea, 2000). There are also governmental regulations on the use of animals in research.

─── CRUCIAL TIP ───

Look back to the studies of Pavlov and Skinner in Chapter 2. Could these be carried out today? What about Watson's study on little Albert?

Further implications of ethics

It is worth thinking about how you might meet the different ethical principles above in various types of psychological study, to see the difficulties that can be involved. For example, in research on child development, parents give their informed consent rather than the participants themselves. If research involves studying a group of people together, there are difficulties maintaining confidentiality (since the participants all see each other) and ensuring that people feel that they can withdraw at any time (due to social pressures).

One very important issue that has been raised in recent years is the **power of the researcher**. Psychologists have a lot of power over participants in two ways. First, in the studies themselves we have seen that participants can feel pressured into doing things they are uncomfortable with and can be left feeling bad. For example, you might find yourself revealing more in an interview than you meant to. Secondly, there are broader social implications for participants. Psychologists need to think about how their research portrays people, and what possible impacts it might have if taken up in social policy. Chapter 4 mentions the damaging impact that intelligence testing has had in the past. If we research some group in our society (such as homeless people, single parents or members of a religious group) we have to think carefully about publicising our findings, particularly if they could be used against the group. We need to consider:

- how the research may be interpreted;
- how confident we can be in our findings (validity and reliability); and
- how much power we have over the publicising of the results.

Several of these ethical issues are linked to the problem of objectivity that we will look at in Chapter 4. The power of the researcher means that people may do things in studies that they would not do in 'real life' when they are not being observed. Misleading participants can lead to them trying to figure out the real nature of the study and conform to it, but if participants are not deceived they will know what the study is trying to do and act accordingly. If people get used to the idea that psychological studies often deceive people (through the many popular books and TV programmes about psychology), this may affect the way they act when they, themselves, are participants. This affects the 'external validity' of psychological studies, i.e. whether we can be sure that our results generalise to the real world.

Ethics in applied psychology

These ethical issues apply to research in both pure and applied psychology. They also need to be considered by professional psychologists applying psychology to people. For example, clinical and counselling psychologists must keep the confidentiality of their clients.

Here are three further issues that practising applied psychologists need to consider in terms of ethical conduct, including examples of areas that are particularly controversial.

The power of the psychologist

Like research psychologists with their participants, practising applied psychologists have a lot of power over their clients. This is because professional psychologists are generally seen as 'experts' who are going to solve the problems of their clients. For example, a criminal psychologist is in a position of power when the police ask them to help solve a crime they are struggling with; an occupational psychologist is in a position of power when an organisation calls them in because they are losing money through stress absenteeism.

In no branch of applied psychology is this more the case than in clinical/counselling psychology. In this branch of psychology the client is likely to be very vulnerable because they have been struggling with a problem that has overwhelmed them to such an extent that they have sought outside help. Seeking help for emotional difficulties is still quite stigmatised in our society. The clinical/counselling psychologist has a lot of expert power over the client because they are perceived as having the solution. They also have financial power (the client pays them) and emotional power (they can make the client feel better or worse). There are issues of whether it is possible for the client to give informed consent to therapy in such a situation. It would also be easy for a psychologist in this situation to abuse their power, for example to keep a private client coming to them for longer than necessary for the money, or to use dubious therapies with the client.

One example of this latter problem was the use of aversion therapy in the 1950s and 1960s to 'cure' people of homosexuality (see section 2 of Chapter 2). Homosexuality was classed as a disorder by the American Psychiatric Association Diagnostic and Statistical Manual (DSM-II) until 1973. A more recent example is the debate over 'false memory syndrome' (FMS). It seems that some therapists may well have convinced clients that they have been sexually abused and have hidden the memories deep in their unconscious mind (repression – see section 1 of Chapter 2). There is actually very little evidence that this is possible, but some clients have even taken the supposed abusers to court, causing a great deal of pain for all concerned (Conway, 1997). The controversies also mean that genuine victims of sexual abuse may find even more difficulty in getting help and respect. There is a real danger when applied psychologists come to believe a theory which has not been properly researched (e.g. that people repress memories of painful events). They may convince their clients of the theory because they are searching for anything that explains their negative feelings, and this, in turn, reinforces the psychologist's own beliefs.

The validity of the theories

Related to the above point is the question of validity of the theories used by applied psychologists. When psychologists are in such a position of power, they need to think very carefully about the theories they are applying to people. The theories may actually be harmful, like viewing homosexuality as a disorder or believing in FMS. Alternatively they may just not be valid or effective. In this case, the clients would be paying the applied psychologist money to do something that wasn't actually helpful.

This is an important issue for psychologists who use therapies with clients because there is a lot of debate over the effectiveness of therapies. Much research has found that there is very little difference in the effectiveness of different types of therapy (e.g. psychodynamic, humanist, cognitive and behavioural – Smith and Glass, 1977). If this is the case then how can psychologists justify the theoretical basis of what they are doing? Pennebaker (1997) found that expressing emotions was beneficial, suggesting that perhaps this is what is helpful about all therapies rather than the actual methods used (see Chapter 4). There is still much debate about therapy effectiveness, how this can be ascertained and whether different therapies are more beneficial for certain problems than others.

Validity and effectiveness are important issues for clinical/counselling psychologists to consider when using therapies with people. Another important issue is how to determine whether someone is 'abnormal' or not. As we saw, homosexuality was seen as an abnormality in the past and is no longer perceived that way. This is an example of historical bias (Chapter 4). Rosenhan (1973) carried out studies which suggest that it is very difficult to determine normality/abnormality. He got eight people with no psychological disorder to request appointments at psychiatric hospitals, saying they heard voices saying single words like 'empty' and 'thud'. All these 'pseudo-patients' were admitted to hospital, at which point they ceased to show any false or aberrant behaviour. Despite this, they were kept in for between 9 and 52 days and then discharged with the diagnosis of 'schizophrenia in remission'. In a follow-up study, Rosenhan told psychiatric hospitals that some fake patients might apply for admission over the next month. Of 193 genuine patients who were admitted during that time, staff were confident that 41 were not genuine.

There are serious issues with validity of theories in occupational and educational psychology too, particularly in the area of psychometric testing.

─────────────── CRUCIAL CONCEPT ───────────────

Psychometric testing refers to the measurement of psychological functions such as personality and intelligence (the areas covered by the 'individual differences' branch of pure psychology).

Intelligence tests are controversial because they have frequently been found to be culturally biased. They often draw heavily on the culture in which they were designed, so that people from other cultures do badly (see Chapter 4). Their validity has also been questioned because it is possible to improve scores on them through practice, and they only test certain abilities and are not representative of others. For example, they generally do not measure practical sense, ability to solve everyday challenges or aspects of 'emotional intelligence' such as social skills, empathy and self-management. Despite such difficulties, intelligence tests are still widely used to stream children in schools and as part of the selection process in organisations.

Personality tests are controversial for similar reasons. They are often culturally biased and there are questions over whether they are valid and reliable (see Chapter 4), particularly since they are based on so many different theories of personality which propose different numbers and types of personality traits. For example, Eysenck's Personality Inventory (EPI) is based on three dimensions (neuroticism, extraversion and psychoticism), while Cattell's 16PF measures 16 personality factors. The conditions under which people take personality tests have been found to influence their score and people can lie on tests to show themselves in a good light. Personality tests are used in assessment in many organisations, often because they seem more objective and less prone to bias than interviews. However, the evidence for their predictive value is frequently exaggerated. Personality tests generally do not predict well whether someone is suited to a job. Specific work-sample tests are a more valid way of assessing this. When personality tests are used, the occupational psychologist needs to be trained in administering them and be aware of their limitations.

'Using' psychology on people

The final ethical consideration in applying psychology is about the potential abuse of psychological theories that **have** been found to be effective. For example, psychological findings about how to persuade and influence people, such as Milgram's study or the psychology of behaviour modification, could be used in the following, ethically controversial ways:

- to promote products in advertising (especially potentially dangerous ones such as cigarettes and alcohol);

- to help political parties to get people to vote for them;
- in wartime propaganda – this often involves portraying the enemy as simply evil so people will not question the acts their country is involved in (see Baumeister's fascinating 1997 book on evil).

Applied psychologists need to consider the ethics of the work they are involved with and of using persuasion techniques in general.

─────────────── CRUCIAL TIP ───────────────

Read up on the psychology of persuasion and social influence in an introductory or social psychology textbook. Think about the ways in which such techniques could be used unethically. How could we prevent this?

Section summary

There are many ethical problems involved in carrying out psychological research on humans and animals. Ethical guidelines have been put in place to try to minimise these, and psychologists need to consider the implications of each of these guidelines when conducting research. Ethical issues also need to be taken account of by practising applied psychologists when dealing with clients/organisations.

Quick test

List the ethical principles in psychological research. Relating this back to *Big Brother*, say how well you think this TV programme meets each of the principles. If you saw *The Experiment* (the BBC TV version of Zimbardo's study) you could consider that too. Should TV producers have to conform to the same set of ethical guidelines as psychologists do? What do you think of the applied psychologists (such as counselling psychologists) who have appeared on *Big Brother* and similar programmes giving their opinions? The July 2002 edition of *The Psychologist* magazine includes a discussion of these issues and a report from the psychologists involved in *The Experiment*.

Section 5

End of chapter assessment

Questions

These questions relate to the three assessment targets set at the beginning of this chapter. If you can answer them effectively you are in a good position to get good credit in assessments or examinations.

1. Is it helpful for psychologists to be divided into pure scientists and applied practitioners?
2. Outline the major areas of applied psychology, detailing the work such psychologists conduct.
3. Imagine that you are carrying out an experiment to see how quickly people respond to emotional and non-emotional words on a computer screen (the emotional Stroop task, Matthews and MacLeod, 1985). You want to compare the responses of anxious people to those of non-anxious people. Discuss how you would ensure that the study met each of the BPS's ethical guidelines.

Answers

1. This question requires you to decide on an opinion (yes, no or maybe) and support it throughout your answer. If this was an essay question, you should start with an

introduction stating whether it is helpful, and also giving some historical context about why psychology has been broken down in this way. The rest of your essay would be points justifying the position you have taken. If you decide that the distinction is useful, you could write about the two types of psychology to show that they are different, giving examples of each. If you decide that the distinction is not useful, you could display awareness of the overlap between pure and applied psychology and some of the drawbacks of splitting psychology up in this way (lack of communication, undervaluing applied psychology, etc.). A good answer would show awareness of the alternative position to the one you have chosen. For example, if you decide that the distinction isn't useful you would start by explaining why people might think it is, and then outline some of the problems with this, before reaching an overall conclusion. If you were asked this as a short-answer question in an exam, you would just need to get in the points covered in the relevant part of section 1.

2. This is a fairly straightforward question. If it was a short-answer exam question you should just bullet point the main areas of applied psychology covered in section 3, giving a couple of sentences for each describing the type of work involved. If this was an essay question, you should start by explaining what applied psychology is, and then explain how it is broken down, giving each of the areas a separate subsection (with subheading). For each one you could give a fairly thorough description, preferably with examples to illustrate the type of work carried out. In the conclusion a good essay would also mention additional, more recent, areas of applied psychology such as health and sport psychology. You should also point out that there is overlap between the areas and that applied psychologists may conduct research too, perhaps giving some examples. For exam revision purposes it would be useful to make sure that you could answer the same question about pure psychology.

3. If this is an essay question rather than an exam question, it would be useful to find out a bit more about the study it mentions (Matthews and MacLeod, 1985). This study is mentioned in the Crucial Study Text on cognitive psychology. However, the question gives you enough information to be able to tackle it in an exam, because it is really asking what you know about ethics, not what you know about the emotional Stroop task.

A good answer to this question would have a general introduction, followed by subheadings for each of the BPS's ethical principles for research on human participants. Each subsection would clearly explain the principle, and would consider the potential difficulties in applying them to this study and what the researcher would have to take into consideration. There would then be a general conclusion about whether the study could meet the principles, and which ones would need most consideration. For example, you might want to consider the possibility of the study upsetting participants, and the issues involved in studying a vulnerable group (people with anxiety).

Section 6

Further reading and research

If you want to read more on the crucial studies mentioned in this chapter, you can find summaries and discussions of the original papers in:

Banyard, P. and Grayson, A. (2000) *Introducing Psychological Research.* Basingstoke: Palgrave.

All introductory psychology textbooks cover the areas of pure psychology in depth. There is a nice, brief overview of some of the main areas in:

Butler, G. and McManus, F. (1998) *Psychology: A Very Short Introduction.* Oxford: Oxford University Press.

The 'Applying Psychology To...' series of books is excellent for more information on the various applied areas (Harrower, 1998; Hayward, 1996; Banyard, 1996; Woods, 1998). The following two books are good general introductions to applied psychology. The first covers issues in applied psychology while the second goes through the different branches in detail.

Hartley, J. and Branthwaite, A. (2000) *The Applied Psychologist*. Buckingham: Open University Press.
Coolican, H., Cassidy, T., Chercher, A., Harrower, J., Penny, G., Sharp, R., Walley, M. and Westbury, T. (1996) *Applied Psychology*. London: Hodder & Staughton.

For more information on ethics, see the British Psychological Society Code of Conduct, Ethical Principles and Guidelines, available on the Internet at www.bps.org.uk.

The most recent guidelines on animal research are covered in: Lea, Stephen E. F. (2000) 'Towards an ethical use of animals', *The Psychologist,* 13(11), 556–7.

Two good books on ethics are:

Cardwell, M. (1999) *Ethical Issues in Psychology.* London: Routledge.
Kimmel, A. J. (1996) *Ethical Issues in Behavioural Research.* Oxford: Blackwell.

Chapter 4
Themes and debates in psychological research

Chapter summary

Over the years psychologists have generally seen their discipline as a science, like chemistry or physics. Most psychologists adopt the scientific method, seeing it as the best way of discriminating between theories to determine which best explain human behaviour. Psychologists have also tried very hard to get other people to see psychology as a science. Along with their belief in the value of the scientific method, this may also be partly due to the fact that, in our society, sciences are perceived as much more hard-nosed and rigorous than other disciplines, so people may well believe in them more and trust their results. It may also be because traditionally sciences have been given more money than other disciplines by governments and funding bodies.

Because psychology involves human beings studying other human beings, it can be susceptible to biases and errors, some of which are not there when people study something like chemicals or electricity, and which may lead people to question its position as an 'objective science'.

In this chapter, we consider what a science is, and whether psychology can be said to be one. We examine some of the problems that psychology encounters because it involves humans studying humans. Finally, we look at possible alternatives to seeing psychology as a science that have been put forward over the years.

Assessment targets

Target 1: Understanding what a science is and how psychology fits into this
Sciences share various aims and ways of theorising and carrying out research. This chapter will help you to understand these and see how psychology fits in. Particularly you will consider the need to be 'objective' and issues around the measurement of human behaviour. Question 1 at the end of the chapter tests this.

Target 2: Explaining biases in psychological research
There have been many biases inherent in past psychological research. Two of the main ones are the 'androcentric' bias and the 'ethnocentric' bias, meaning that psychology has been biased in favour of men, and people from white, Western societies. This chapter will give examples of these biases so that you can understand the problems they have caused. Question 2 at the end of the chapter tests your grasp of these biases.

Target 3: Understanding problems inherent in studying human beings
In addition to general biases, there are several difficulties inherent in a discipline where both researchers and participants are humans. This chapter will help you to understand some of these problems, such as demand characteristics, their potential impact on the validity of psychological research, and how psychologists have reacted to this. Question 3 at the end of the chapter tests your understanding of these problems.

Target 4: Describing alternative positions to psychology being a science
Some individuals and groups of psychologists over the years have disputed whether psychology should be seen as a science at all. This chapter will outline the main current alternative position: the 'new paradigm' psychology that has emerged since the 1970s. You should also refer back to the 'humanist' approach of the 1950s and 1960s (Chapter 2).

Question 4 at the end of the chapter tests you on these alternatives within the context of whether psychology is a science.

How will you be assessed on this?

The issue of whether psychology is a science is one of the big debates in psychology, so you are very likely to be asked questions about it in both coursework essays and exams. It is important that you know what a science is, and how psychology fits into the definition of a science (section 1). It is also useful to be able to give examples of problems with measuring human characteristics and difficulties with psychology being 'objective' and 'generalisable' (sections 2 and 3), and 'alternative' views some psychologists have put forward to psychology being a science (section 4). This is quite a tricky topic because it involves a lot of long words, like 'objective', 'replicable' and even 'hypothetico-deductive'! Don't be put off by this: all these terms have very basic explanations. The important thing is to be able to understand the issues involved. It doesn't matter if you can't remember the exact words, but I have included them all as 'crucial concepts' to help with this.

Section 1

Is psychology a science?

In this section we look at what a science is, and how psychology fits into this.

What is a science?

To understand how psychology can be seen to be a science, we first need to understand clearly what science is. When I teach this to students I always start off by asking them to think back to when they took science lessons in school. This helps them to get their head round what science involves. Try this now. Think back to your GCSEs (or equivalent). When you took chemistry, physics or biology, what kinds of things did you do in class? Think of lots of answers to this question. Then come to some conclusions about what a science is, writing down a list of things that sciences try to do.

Apart from memories of white lab coats, test tubes and Bunsen burners, you may have come up with some of the following answers to the question:

- **Measurement.** Sciences measure things. You might remember testing the temperature of water when it reaches boiling point, or measuring weights and heights of objects. Scientists try to measure things as accurately as possible.
- **Explanation.** Scientists try to explain what causes things to happen. Think of Newton when the apple fell on him. Scientists believe that every effect has a cause. Newton came up with the theory of gravity to explain why things always fall to earth when we drop them.
- **Experiments.** Science uses experiments to test theories. You might remember the chemistry teacher dropping a small amount of sodium into a big tank of water and then putting a lit match near it. You could see the sodium fizzing around as it reacted with the water and hear the 'pop' noise of the match, showing that hydrogen gas was being given off. This experiment tests the theory that sodium reacts with water to give off hydrogen.
- **Control.** Scientific experiments are very controlled. You would always measure the exact amount of each substance in a chemical experiment with very precise equipment such as electric scales and measuring tubes.
- **Repetition.** Science often repeats experiments several times to check the results. You'll probably remember that when you carried out experiments in class everyone

came up with slightly different answers because small errors in measurement are almost unavoidable. Generally, you would measure things many times and take an average (mean) of the measurements. However, repeating the study several times would show you that results did not change drastically. For example, if you measure the temperature at which water boils, the mercury in the thermometer will always be at, or very close to, one hundred degrees centigrade.

So sciences aim to measure things accurately in order to develop theories that explain why things happen (cause and effect). To do this they use controlled scientific experiments, which can be repeated over and over to check their results. You'll see in this section that psychology also tries to do these things, but that there can be difficulties.

--- CRUCIAL CONCEPT ---

The word **empirical** is often used to mean the same thing as scientific. It means measuring things as accurately as possible. Empiricism is the approach that collects information through our senses (sight, sound, etc.) rather than relying on faith or what other people say.

--- CRUCIAL TIP ---

Before you read on about whether psychology is scientific, ask yourself what you think. Now you know what a science involves, how well do you think psychology fits into this? Think about psychological studies that you have come across and branches of psychology that we have covered earlier in this book. Do they fit the definition of a science or not? Overall, would you say that psychology is a science?

Psychology and objectivity

The question of whether psychology is a science or not is tied to the question of whether it can be objective.

--- CRUCIAL CONCEPT ---

Objective means not being influenced by personal feelings or opinions. It is the opposite of **subjective**, which means looking at things from a personal point of view.

Most sciences are seen as being objective because scientists can measure the things that they are studying without their own opinions or feelings getting in the way. If a physicist is measuring the electricity running through a wire, it doesn't matter how they are feeling that day or what they want the results to be, 10 volts is always 10 volts. Being unbiased and objective is an ideal, but all sciences are affected by the fact that it is humans doing the observation, and humans are never completely objective. For example, an astronomer may not be completely objective when observing something that could be a new planet. They might want to be the one to make the new discovery, and may therefore see it as a planet even if there is evidence that it might be something less interesting. On a recent television documentary a scientist spoke about his theory that much of the water on the earth originally came from comets. However, there was evidence that the water on comets was different to the water in the sea. This presented problems for his theory. He spoke about the importance of not becoming too attached to a theory. This can be difficult though, when a scientist has worked all their life on a particular idea.

Objectivity can also be a problem in psychology. Psychologists are often involved in measuring things about people that are nowhere near as exact as something like electricity, height, weight or temperature. For example, if a psychologist is measuring an aspect of personality, the way in which they define it and measure it may depend on: their background, the historical time they are working at, the kind of person they are, and all sorts of other factors (see section 2). The fact that psychologists are human, with human feelings, beliefs and biases, and the fact that they are studying human beings rather than something more exact like chemicals or electric circuits, can cause problems for psychology being seen as an 'objective science'.

Psychology and the scientific method

We saw that one of the main things involved in science is the approach used, the 'scientific method'. This is the way in which scientists collect data and test theories, often through the use of experiments. Most psychologists adopt the scientific method in order to distinguish between good and bad theories. So an important part of the debate over whether psychology is a science is the issue of whether it can use the 'scientific method', and whether data can be collected in an unbiased, objective way.

There are three main aspects of the scientific method which aim to ensure objectivity. These are: experimental control, operational definitions and replicability.

CRUCIAL CONCEPT

Experimental control is there to help us to find out what causes things. It means holding everything else that may affect the object of interest constant, so that we can determine cause and effect.

Cause and effect

To consider the issues around cause and effect, we will look at the example of media violence research. There has been a lot of research in psychology to see whether watching violence on TV causes people to become aggressive. Psychologists want to see whether the possible cause (TV violence) leads to the effect (aggression) – see Figure 4.1.

To discover whether TV violence causes aggression scientifically, we might carry out the following experiment in our laboratory. We would divide people into two groups. One would watch a violent film on TV and the other a non-violent film. Afterwards we would measure how aggressive each group was. If the group who saw the violent film were more aggressive than the other group, we could say that TV violence had caused them to become aggressive.

However, in order to be sure of our results, we would have to use 'experimental control' to keep everything else that might affect the results constant.

For example, we couldn't show one group of people the film *Bambi* and the other group *Terminator 2*. There are a lot of differences between *Bambi* and *Terminator 2* besides the levels of violence. We couldn't be sure whether the increase in aggression was due to violence or to one of the other differences (*T2* being more realistic, action-packed, etc.). To be controlled, we would have to show the two groups films that were identical in every way, except that one would have the violent scenes replaced with non-violent ones.

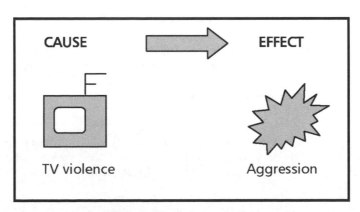

Figure 4.1 Cause and effect

We would also need experimental control in allocating participants to each of the two groups. We'd have to make sure that the people in each group were as similar as possible. If we didn't do this, we might end up with, for example, more men, or more young people in one group than the other. If that happened, we wouldn't know whether it was the film that made them more aggressive, or something to do with their gender, age or other characteristics.

As you can see, ensuring control in psychological experiments is a complicated process, and involves thinking about every possibility.

CRUCIAL CONCEPT

Operational definitions are where we define exactly what particular terms mean so they can be measured and quantified (given a number).

For example, if we want to measure aggression, as in the above experiment, we would have to agree about what aggression means, and how to measure if someone is aggressive. Plus we would have to make sure we were using the same definitions as other psychologists who have worked in this area. In psychology, aggression has been measured in various ways, for example: questionnaires asking how people are feeling, observations of whether people hit an inflatable toy, and measurement of whether people give others electric shocks when presented with the opportunity. Would all psychologists agree that these things are aggression? If we ask people to measure how aggressive they are feeling on a scale of 1 to 10, would a 7 on that scale mean the same thing for every person?

CRUCIAL CONCEPT

Validity is a related concept to this. It refers to how far a measure assesses what it was intended to measure. Do aggression questionnaires really measure aggression? Do they all measure the same thing? We generally want studies to have validity and reliability (see later).

CRUCIAL CONCEPT

Replicability means that the same study could be done again on a different group of people or in a different context with the same result.

For example, if TV violence leads to aggression, we would expect the study to be replicable on different age groups and people from different backgrounds or cultures. We would also expect to find that people were as aggressive after watching a violent film in their own home as they were in the laboratory. One problem with media violence research is that it is not always replicable. Studies on different groups and in different contexts have found different results. Some find that media violence does have an effect and some find that it does not (see Harrower, 1998, for further details).

CRUCIAL CONCEPT

The **hypothetico-deductive method** is the scientific method for testing theories (originally outlined by the philosopher, Popper). Particularly important is the formulation of an explicit hypothesis (a prediction of what will happen) from a more general theory. Empirical investigations test the hypothesis (to see if the prediction is true). If the prediction works, the hypothesis is retained and there is evidence to support the original theory. If the prediction does not work, the hypothesis is refuted and there is evidence against the theory. An alternative theory may be sought.

Figure 4.2 displays the hypothetico-deductive method. This is the scientific method that psychologists apply when carrying out research. To illustrate this process, I will explain how one psychologist, James Pennebaker (1997), used this method in his area of research: expressing emotions.

Pennebaker started with 'observing regularities'. He observed that many people express their emotions, writing about them in diaries, talking through them with counsellors or

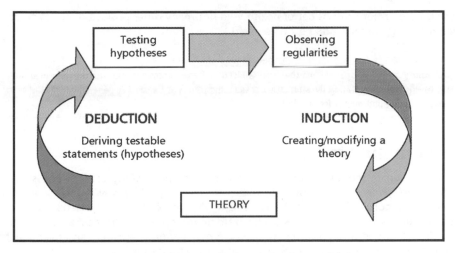

Figure 4.2 The hypothetico-deductive method

speaking about them in the context of religious ritual. From this observation, he went through a process of 'induction'. He created the theory that expressing emotions was good for people. Then he went through the process of 'deduction'. He derived a testable statement from his theory (a hypothesis). He hypothesised that people who expressed their emotions would have better health than those who did not. He tested this hypothesis by questioning people who had been through a traumatic experience, such as bereavement. He found a regularity: people who had talked about their feelings following their experience were in much better health than those who had not.

So you can see that Pennebaker went through the whole cycle displayed in the diagram. He did not stop there though. Finding out that people who talk about their feelings are in better health does not prove 'cause and effect'. It could be that talking about feelings leads to good health, or it could be that people in good health are more likely to talk about their feelings. Or there may some completely unrelated difference between the groups of people that causes one to be healthy and talk more, and the other to be unhealthy and talk less (such as whether they live in the country or town).

─────────────── CRUCIAL TIP ───────────────

Be careful not to confuse **correlation** with **causation**. Just because someone finds a relationship between two things (correlation), does not mean that we can tell that one caused the other (causation). Further studies have to be carried out to demonstrate cause and effect, and to show the direction of this relationship.

Pennebaker went through the process of 'induction' again, modifying his theory to one stating that expressing emotions actually **causes** better health. Through the process of deduction he hypothesised that people who were given an opportunity to express their emotions would be in better health a few months down the line than people who were not. He tested this with experiments. Students were allocated to two groups. One wrote about their emotions for an hour every day for a week, the other wrote about trivial things, like what they'd had for breakfast. A few months later the group who had written about their feelings were in much better health than the other group: they had been to the doctor fewer times and their immune systems were working better. From this, Pennebaker concluded that expressing emotions does cause better health.

So you can see from this example that psychology can follow the scientific method. Going back to the issue of 'replicability', the 'hypothetico-deductive' cycle enables us to keep on testing and re-testing our theories. This repetition means that we can be confident that the results are reliable. Many people have replicated Pennebaker's study and found that expressing emotions causes better health, and has many other positive effects. You could even have a go at replicating it on yourself!

CRUCIAL CONCEPT

Reliability means that people find the same results on different occasions and with different measures, i.e. psychologists replicating the study will get the same results as before. We generally want studies to have reliability and validity (see earlier).

Section summary

We have seen in the latter part of this section that psychology can use the scientific method. However, we have also seen that there can be problems with this. Maintaining experimental control is difficult. Measurement of psychological phenomena can also be problematic, as we have shown with the example of aggression. In the next two sections we will look at two further problems: biases in psychological research, and the impact of being studied on how participants in psychological studies behave.

Quick test

Write a list of ways in which psychology meets the criteria for being a science, with examples if you can think of them.

Section 2

Bias in psychological research

This section looks at some of the biases that psychologists may be prone to, which affect their ability to be 'objective' researchers.

CRUCIAL TIP

Before we begin this section, try writing down the names of all the psychologists you have come across in your lectures and reading. Now ask yourself two questions. How many of those people are white? How many are male?

Ethnocentrism

CRUCIAL CONCEPT

Ethnocentrism means being steeped in the values of your own ethnic group, and assuming that those values are 'normal' and 'natural' and that cultures that do not share them are not 'normal'.

Critics have accused psychology of being ethnocentric because the western values of American and European life shape many of its theories and studies. There are several different, but related, criticisms.

- **The western view is the prevailing view.** Smith and Bond (1993) found that 64 per cent of psychological research world-wide is American. They looked at psychology textbooks and found that most of the studies mentioned were American. Often research that does not fit the prevailing (western) view is not published.

- **Research participants are an unrepresentative group.** A great deal of American psychological research is carried out on undergraduate students, because they are readily available to psychologists working in universities. For example, Tedeshi et al. (1985) found that 70 per cent of social psychology studies involved undergraduate participants. Psychology students in America participate in psychological experiments to gain course credits (Krupat and Garonzik, 1994). Most undergraduate students are white, young and educated. Therefore they are not representative of even American people as a whole, let alone people in other cultures.

- **Generalising from western participants is problematic.** Despite this, psychologists have often carried out research in the West and then assumed that the theories based on this research will apply to all humans. Famous studies that have sometimes failed to be replicated in other cultures include Milgram's (1974) obedience to authority research (see Chapter 3), and Sherif et al.'s (1956) Robbers' Cave studies on intergroup conflict which found that American schoolboys displayed aggression and prejudice when they were divided into groups and put in competition against each other.

- **Psychology often assumes the superiority of western values.** Psychologists have also often assumed that things that are held to be positive or negative in the West will be the same for all cultures. For example, many western psychologists have seen 'independence' as being something important for humans to achieve. Many psychological theories place a lot of emphasis on becoming independent and see being dependent on others as psychologically bad (e.g. Erikson's theory of lifespan development and Maslow's hierarchy of needs – see Chapter 2). However, many eastern 'collectivist' cultures value self-sacrifice and honouring the family or community rather than independence and western 'individualism'.

- **Psychology has been racist.** Howitt and Owasu-Bempah (1994) state that psychology in the past has been explicitly racist (see crucial study below). There is no scientific evidence for the concept of 'race', i.e. the assumption that people of different colours or from different geographical locations have distinct biological features and essential characteristics (Richards, 1996). Howitt and Owasu-Bempah further argue that racism is still present in psychology today, but in a subtler form. Psychology still uses words that suggest that other cultures are 'different' or 'deficient' and rarely supports research that furthers understanding of non-western cultures.

--- CRUCIAL STUDY ---

Intelligence testing is one of the most controversial topics in psychology, largely because the results of such tests have been used as evidence of racial differences, supporting racist policies. I would highly recommend Stephen Jay Gould's famous (1982) paper about this called 'A nation of morons', from his (1981) book *The Mismeasure of Man*. Here is a brief summary:

Gould describes how intelligence tests were introduced in America to assess army recruits in the First World War. The tests were seen as a way of getting psychology to be recognised as a rigorous science. The research found that the average intelligence of recruits decreased with the darkness of their skin, and that blacks had the lowest scores, perpetuating racist attitudes towards black people in America. Immigrants to the US, including Jews, also generally obtained low scores. Because they believed intelligence to be completely inherited (see the nature–nurture debate in Chapter 5), the researchers concluded that different racial groups had different levels of 'natural' intelligence. These findings had a major impact on the immigration debate. Eugenicists used the findings to argue that 'inferior' immigrants were bringing down the level of national intelligence. An Act was passed in 1924 limiting immigration. This prevented approximately six million Europeans from entering America between then and the start of the Second World War, condemning them to the Holocaust (Gross, 1999). Gould argues that the assumption that intelligence tests measure general innate intelligence is one of the most shameful things in the history of psychology.

Some of the main flaws with the tests were:

- They were not carried out properly, so many people ended up taking the wrong test. Often illiterate people took the test meant for literate people and were not re-tested. Even if they took the correct test, illiterate and foreign-born recruits would have to use a pencil, write numbers and generally take part in a procedure they were completely unfamiliar with.
- Foreign-born recruits' test scores improved the more years they had been resident in America, suggesting that intelligence was not completely innate, but there was at least some impact of environment.

Many of the questions tested familiarity with American culture rather than 'native intellectual ability'. Try answering the following questions yourself:

- Crisco is a: patent medicine, disinfectant, toothpaste, food product?
- Washington is to Adams as first is to ... ?
- There were also pictures asking people to fill in the missing part of a gun, light bulb or playing card.

——— CRUCIAL TIP ———

Always try to remember some specific examples like the ones given here from the intelligence tests. These really help to support your arguments in essays.

Androcentrism

——— CRUCIAL CONCEPT ———

Androcentrism means 'male-centred' or 'dominated by male standards'.

Psychology has also been accused of gender bias. Psychological research has traditionally been dominated by male researchers and has been carried out on mainly male participants. It has often ignored women, assuming that findings from men will also apply to women. For example, research into unemployment and retirement has often used all-male participants. Clearly findings on these topics will not simply generalise to women. There has also been very little research into predominately female experiences such as pregnancy, rape, menopause and the experience of women in the workplace.

Some psychologists have explicitly seen women as inferior to men (see Freud's accounts of gender in Chapter 2 and the crucial study below).

——— CRUCIAL STUDY ———

Kohlberg (1968) researched the development of moral reasoning. He gave problems to boys of different ages and asked them to say what they would do and why. One example is the 'Heinz dilemma' where a man, Heinz, cannot afford the over-inflated price that is being charged for the drug that would save his wife's life, so he steals the drug. From the boys' answers, Kohlberg concluded that we progress through the following stages of moral development:

• 'pre-conventional morality' – avoiding punishment and following rules that we, ourselves, benefit from;
• 'conventional morality' – pleasing others and following societal laws;
• 'post-conventional morality' – trying to achieve 'the greatest good for the greatest number', or even following our own, carefully thought-out, ethical principles.

Kohlberg assumed that men were superior in terms of moral ability, and that women could not reach the high stages of moral reasoning, despite not having actually studied any women.

Evaluation

Gilligan and Attanucci (1988) argued that the two genders have different ways of assessing moral dilemmas, based on their different life experiences. Boys tend to judge morality in terms of justice and girls in terms of caring for the needs of others. Therefore Kohlberg's stages based entirely on men inevitably misrepresent women's moral thinking.

Some have also criticised psychology because so many of its studies look for psychological differences between the sexes. They argue that we should look for sex similarities as well as differences, because although men and women are physically different, the psychological similarities between the sexes far outweigh the differences. Research that finds a gender difference is more likely to be published than that which does not. Also, psychologists should consider socialisation as well as biological sex to explain gender differences (see the nature–nurture debate in Chapter 5). For example, early research into conformity found that women conformed more than men; this was used to fuel the view that women were naturally inferior to men in intelligence. Later research found that men and women conform equally and that conforming has to do with how much familiarity the person has with the conformity task (Sistrunk and McDavid, 1971). Early research used tasks that were more familiar to men than women because of the way they were brought up, for example tasks involving machinery. Many researchers looked no further because the findings confirmed their sexist assumptions (Hogg and Vaughan, 2002).

There are now feminist psychologists who question the gender bias in previous research and carry out research on women's experiences (see Chapter 2). Many feminist psychologists critique the whole notion of psychology as a science (see section 4 of this chapter). It is important to remember that gender bias can be harmful to both men and women. For example, theories suggesting that women are better at childcare than men could be used to support policies keeping women out of the workplace, and also ones preventing men from being the primary carers of children.

Linked to androcentrism is 'heterosexism', which is the view that anything other than heterosexuality is abnormal. This can be seen in the theories of Freud and Erikson. Erikson's model of lifespan development includes seeking 'relationships with a partner of the opposite sex'. A 'lesbian and gay psychology' section of the BPS was set up in 1999.

CRUCIAL TIP

For a discussion about why psychology might need a 'lesbian and gay' section, see Kitzinger et al.'s paper in *The Psychologist* (November, 1998), and the letters page in subsequent issues.

Historical bias

A further, slightly more complicated bias in psychological research could be termed 'historical bias'. This is the fact that the psychological phenomena that are seen as interesting, and the way we measure them, change over time.

An example of this is 'authoritarianism'. This has been seen differently at different historical times: Nazi psychologists in the 1930s saw it as a positive thing, US researchers more recently saw it as a negative thing. Authoritarianism as we define it today might also have been seen as a very positive thing in Victorian times. Just after the Korean war, American psychologists tested people to see how persuadable they were. This was due to fears of people being 'brainwashed'. People who were less easy to persuade were perceived more positively, even though resistance to persuasion could be seen as being a very similar thing to authoritarianism.

So there have been differences over time and culture in whether authoritarianism is regarded as positive or negative. Authoritarianism has also been measured in different ways at different times. Try saying whether you agree or disagree with these statements from two 1950s scales and asking yourself whether they measure authoritarianism as we would define it today:

- After the war, we may expect a crime wave; the control of gangsters and ruffians will become a major social problem.
- Although many people may scoff, it may yet be shown that astrology can explain a lot of things.
- Divorce laws should be altered to make divorce easier.
- Birth control, except when recommended by a doctor, should be made illegal.
- It would be best to keep coloured people in their own districts and schools in order to prevent too much contact with whites.

(Taken from Richards, 1996.)

Agreeing with any of these statements in the 1950s meant that you had an authoritarian attitude. I'm sure you can see that some of these questions are meaningless today or the context has changed, and most would not indicate what we now see as authoritarianism. For example, believing in astrology would probably be a sign of being open-minded, if not somewhat gullible. Try thinking up questions that would measure authoritarianism in Britain today. You will probably base them around quite different topics, like green issues or drug use.

So what authoritarianism is varies over time, as well as whether we perceive it as positive or negative. We can even question whether a stable attitude called 'authoritarianism' exists at all. Graham Richards (1996) points out that 'everything that can be measured does not necessarily exist'. He argues that psychology actually invents many of the things that it studies. For example, nobody had an Oedipus complex before Freud, nobody had a high IQ before 1914, and people did not 'suffer from stress' until very recent times. The concept of authoritarianism would not have meant much before the nineteenth century. People might have been more interested in how devout someone was, or whether they had heretical beliefs.

These historical shifts in the perception of phenomena are further problems for the idea of psychology as an objective science. We tend to view things from a 'present-centred' perspective, assuming that the things that we talk about today exist and are important. Studying historical and cultural variations can help us to see that it may not be as simple as this. Hayes (1999) states that the theories and methods that become popular tend to be the ones that fit the 'zeitgeist' (the social and cultural climate of the time).

CRUCIAL TIP

In its aim to be scientific, psychology has often tried to put numbers to things. Such measurement is relatively simple when we are looking at reaction times in cognitive psychology (e.g. how long it takes someone to read a word when it flashes up on a computer screen – see Chapter 3). However, it becomes much more problematic when we try to study complex psychological phenomena like intelligence, personality, attitudes and aggression. Cultural, historical and personal biases can all have an influence. We can see that psychologists' own values come into any research that they do to some extent. To ask a question like 'what is the link between race and intelligence?' we are assuming that 'race', 'intelligence' and connections between them exist and are important.

Section summary

Psychology has been accused of being biased because:

- most researchers have been white males;
- most participants in studies have been white males;
- heterosexual white males still tend to be presented as the norm in human behaviour against which everyone else is compared;
- psychological phenomena may be seen in different ways at different points in time.

These all present problems for psychology being seen as an objective, unbiased, science.

Quick test

Give three examples of bias in psychology: one of culture bias, one of gender bias and one of historical bias.

Section 3

The impact of the research situation

There are several potential problems in psychological research to do with the fact that it involves human researchers investigating human participants, in addition to the biases covered in the previous section. This section looks at how participants and researchers behave in psychological studies.

We have seen several problems caused by the fact that humans are carrying out the research in psychology: they are vulnerable to bias due to their culture, gender and the historical time they are living in. Now we will look at a few problems caused by the fact that the subjects of psychological studies are also humans. Since the 1960s, psychologists have studied what is known as 'the social psychology of the experiment': the way that the experimental situation affects those involved.

Orne (1962) found that people in experimental situations would do things that they would be very unlikely to do in daily life. For example, they would spend hours adding up long lists of figures, only to tear up all their results later on. They would pick up a supposedly poisonous snake, stick their hand into 'fuming nitric acid' and even throw this into the experimenter's face. This is probably because they knew that the experimenter would not really put them at risk; they went along with anything so as not to 'spoil' the experiment.

In fact, participants in psychological studies often try to work out the experimental hypothesis. This is so that they can do one of the following:

- conform to the hypothesis, to 'help out' the researcher;
- mess up the hypothesis;
- try to act as normally as possible in the situation, because they know the experimental 'game'; or
- be very defensive, to try to stop the experimenter getting at 'hidden truths' about them. This comes from the common perception that psychologists can read minds or analyse people.

Participants in psychological studies also often try to behave in a way that is socially desirable: they want to be seen in a positive light, so they may not admit to having, say, negative emotions or prejudices. This is not just a problem for laboratory experiments. The 'Hawthorn effect' shows that people in any situation behave differently when they know they are being observed. For example, if a psychologist goes into a workplace, workers may become more motivated and productive, not because of anything the psychologist has done, but simply because they are there.

Experimenters can leave cues about the purpose of the study without meaning to. Because they know what the hypothesis is, they may inadvertently encourage participants to conform to it. Rosenthal carried out several studies in which he randomly allocated rats, or even children, to two groups. He then told experimenters that one group was brighter than the other, and got them to carry out studies getting the rats (or children!) to learn. The experimenters always obtained better learning from the 'bright' group; their expectations somehow produced improvement even though there was no real difference between the two groups. These 'experimenter effects', along with the expectations of participants in psychology experiments, are collectively known as 'demand characteristics'.

CRUCIAL CONCEPT

Demand characteristics are the features of a study that make the participants behave in unusual ways or ways in which they would not behave in any other situation (see also Samuel and Bryant's 1984 study in section 2 of Chapter 3).

These issues combine with the problem that most participants are undergraduate students, and also that the kind of people who volunteer to take part in psychological studies are generally quite different to people in general (e.g. more easily influenced and neurotic – Ora, 1965). All these things create difficulties for psychologists in generalising the results of their studies. If we know that people behave abnormally in psychological studies then we cannot draw any conclusions from them about the ways in which people behave in the 'real world'. This presents a threat to a certain type of validity, external validity, which is the extent to which any relationship found can be generalised beyond the specific circumstances of the study. If this is low, it is difficult to see the usefulness of the results.

CRUCIAL TIP

The issues covered here tie in with ethical considerations, especially those about deceiving participants and harm. Look back over section 4 of Chapter 3 to revise this and to remind yourself of the link. Ethical considerations often mean that psychologists cannot carry out perfect 'scientific' research.

Psychologists employ various methods to reduce such demand characteristics. For example, they reduce experimenter effects by using 'double blind' procedures, where neither the participant nor the person carrying out the study knows what the hypothesis is. To stop the participant from guessing the real nature of the story, psychologists may use cover stories (pretending the experiment is about something else), or they may include additional tasks or material so it is hard for the participant to guess which part of the experiment is important. In cognitive psychology, material may be presented subliminally (below conscious awareness). To avoid the problem of using certain groups of people, psychologists may carry out their studies on specific, relevant groups (e.g. children, people with a certain disorder, people in a certain workforce). They also use specific techniques to get a representative sample of the population they are interested in (see the research methods book in the Crucial Study Text series for more details about these).

Section summary

Participants may often act differently in psychological studies to the ways they would act in 'real life' and experimenters may unintentionally introduce biases into the research situation. These issues present problems for psychology being seen as an objective science whose findings can be generalised beyond the specific situation of the psychological study itself. Many contemporary psychologists are aware of these limitations to their methods and carefully consider the options for overcoming them.

Quick test

List and explain the different types of 'demand characteristic' that can interfere with psychological studies.

Section 4

Alternatives to seeing psychology as a science

The previous three sections have covered many potential problems for psychology being seen as an objective science. In this section, we look at how psychologists have responded to this, and at alternatives to seeing psychology as a science.

First I will summarise the issue as we can now see it (from the previous sections).

There are problems with seeing psychology as a science because:

- applying the scientific method to psychology is difficult, particularly achieving full experimental control;
- operational definitions are problematic because there are historical and cultural variations in what phenomena are seen as important (or even exist) and how we measure them;
- the biases of psychologists themselves can influence their studies and results;
- the situation of the psychological study can cause participants to behave in ways they would not in everyday life.

Many of these present difficulties for external validity: generalising our results beyond the specific situation of the study itself.

Let's go back to our earlier example: the study on the impact of TV violence on aggression. Say we do find, in our laboratory experiment, that people give more 'electric shocks' to someone after watching a violent film than after a non-violent one. How do we know that our measure of aggression (giving electric shocks) is the same thing as real-life aggression (physical and/or verbal abuse)? Also, how do we know whether people will have the same reaction to watching a violent film in their own homes, with their friends or family, that they do in the laboratory, where they know that they are being observed? The laboratory experiment is an artificial situation that isolates people from the usual complex social factors that surround them.

There have been broadly two reactions to these problems in psychology:

1. Make the environment of psychological experiments even more controlled in an attempt to meet the criteria for a science, for example using the double-blind procedures and specific sampling techniques mentioned above. Some psychologists also use computers to model human behaviour in order to study it in a very controlled way.

2. Stop trying to be a science. Instead, use research methods that recognise the interaction between participants, researchers and the situation as an integral part of psychology.

One group of psychologists who took this second perspective were the humanists, back in the 1950s and 1960s. They felt that controlled experimentation was unsuitable for understanding the human experience (see Chapter 2). A more recent group who have come up with an 'alternative' way of doing psychology are the 'new paradigm' researchers. This research began with Harré and Secord in the early 1970s and has become an alternative to scientific psychology. Such research often involves using qualitative rather than quantitative methods.

─────────── CRUCIAL CONCEPT ───────────

Quantitative methods measure human behaviour in numerical ways (putting numbers to things) and then analyse this data with statistics. **Qualitative** researchers are more interested in the meaning of information, so they don't measure things with numbers. For example, experiments and questionnaire scales are generally quantitative. Interviews and observations can be qualitative. Researchers analyse the themes that people talk about in an interview, or the in-depth meaning of the behaviour that they observe.

New paradigm, qualitative research differs from scientific psychological research because:

- It doesn't try to achieve experimental control in the laboratory but studies people in more 'real' situations, like in conversations and public spaces.

- It doesn't put numbers to psychological phenomena but uses open-ended methods to study people in depth, such as discussion groups and diaries.

- It recognises that researchers will have assumptions and biases and tries to be open about these and consider the impact they have on each stage of the research process. The importance of the social, cultural and historical context is also acknowledged. This is known as being 'reflexive'.

- It doesn't deceive participants, but is completely honest and open with them about what the research involves and aims to achieve. It sees participants as 'collaborators' in the research rather than subjects, and builds up an ongoing rapport between them and the researchers (see discussion of deception and researcher power in section 4 of Chapter 3).

Looking back over this chapter, you will see that qualitative research minimises problems with external validity, since it studies people in their natural environment. It is also a particularly ethical way of doing research, since it does not involve deception (see Chapter 3). However, there are issues around the validity and reliability of qualitative research because it does not attempt control or objectivity. It can be difficult to generalise from qualitative research to larger populations of people, since studies are often so detailed that they can practically only be carried out on small numbers of people. Because of this, critics have argued that qualitative research is not useful, since it cannot tell us much about the behaviour of people in general.

There has been heated debate between the proponents of quantitative and qualitative methods in the psychological literature (see *The Psychologist* magazine for January 1996, April 1997 and October 1998). Many argue that psychology should still attempt to be a science, but some feel that it should completely reject this and study humans in 'more appropriate' ways. Some feel that certain branches of psychology can be scientific (e.g. biological, cognitive), whereas others cannot (e.g. social, parts of applied psychology). Finally, some argue that the best way forward may be to mix the best features of both approaches and to take an 'eclectic' approach to understanding human behaviour (Malim and Birch, 1998; Stevenson and Cooper, 1997).

If you look back to Figure 4.2 of the 'hypothetico-deductive' method (in section 1), you will see that 'induction' is a vital part of the scientific method, but most quantitative, 'scientific' psychology focuses on the 'deductive' part of the cycle. Qualitative methods are particularly well suited to inducing theories from observations. So perhaps proper 'scientific' psychology should include both qualitative research and quantitative hypothesis testing. Also, it could be argued that any good science should be reflexive and recognise potential biases.

─────────── CRUCIAL TIP ───────────

Read back over some of the branches of psychology covered in this book. Which ones do you think come closest to meeting the criteria of science?

Section summary

In this section we have reminded ourselves about the various problems with seeing psychology as a science and have considered how scientific psychology, and the most recent alternative perspective, 'new paradigm' research, have responded to these problems.

Quick test

List the ways in which 'new paradigm' qualitative research differs from 'scientific' psychological research.

Section 5

End of chapter assessment

Questions

These questions relate to the four assessment targets set at the beginning of this chapter. If you can answer them effectively you are in a good position to get good credit in assessments or examinations.

1. Describe the scientific method. What problems does psychology face in trying to apply this method?
2. It has been argued that psychology is just the study of white, American, male students. Do you agree with this criticism? Why is it a problem?
3. How might demand characteristics affect the outcome of psychological studies?
4. Kuhn (1962) states that psychology is just a 'pre-science' and that it cannot yet meet the criteria for being a science, because it has no uniting paradigm. Discuss.

Answers

1. Note that there are two parts to this question. The latter part is the main issue, so you want to use more words on this than on the first part.

   First, briefly describe the scientific method as asked. You can use diagrams in psychological essays, so draw the hypothetico-deductive method and explain it briefly, including the need for experimental control, operational definitions and replicability.

   For the second part of the question you could use one of two tactics. You could choose a specific hypothetical example (like the one I chose: TV violence). You could then go through how psychologists could attempt to study this with the scientific method, picking up difficulties they might come up against: how to ensure experimental control, how to measure aggression and how to show a cause–effect relationship. Alternatively, you could go through the various problems (control, definitions, replicability, cause–effect, etc.), explaining each with different examples of problems psychologists have experienced with them in the past. You might also want briefly to explain demand characteristics and how these can cause problems for the scientific method in psychology.

2. This is a bit of a tricky question. You might well look at it, think 'androcentrism and ethnocentrism – I've covered that!', and then go on to write an essay covering everything you know about gender and culture bias. This is where reading the question carefully is very important. Note that it asks you about psychology being the 'study of' white, American, male students. That means that it is asking about the problems of **participants** all being a certain type of person. It is not interested in the more general problems about researchers mostly being white males, with the accompanying biases.

97

Therefore, you need to focus your answer on the problems of participants being a certain kind of person.

Again, this question has two parts: 'is the statement is a valid criticism?' and 'what would the problems be if it were?' You probably want to spend longer on the second part of the question than the first. For the first part you need to support the claim with evidence, citing the work of people like Tedeshi, who found that most research was carried out on undergraduate students. You should also mention findings about research in the past mostly studying men, although you might want to question whether that is still the case today.

For the second part of the essay you need to state clearly that the problem caused by this is one of generalisation of findings. Then go through the difficulties there have been when people have tried to generalise findings from a limited sample to a more general sample, particularly to other cultures and from men to women. You could include examples like Milgram's and Sherif et al.'s studies, which do not always generalise to other cultures, and Kohlberg's study not applying to women.

3. This is a pretty straightforward question so long as you can remember what 'demand characteristics' are! It is definitely worth making sure you revise the meaning of these kinds of terms for exams (see exam advice in the introduction). For this question you have a very clear answer: the main effect of demand characteristics is to undermine the external validity of psychological studies, i.e. our ability to generalise from them to the 'real world'. Make this point clearly in the introduction, then go through the various demand characteristics explaining what they are with examples and how they undermine external validity. Finish off with a conclusion reiterating that the main concern is for external validity. For a really good essay, you might want to draw some wider implications from this for the idea of psychology as an 'objective' science. You could even bring in some alternative ways of doing psychology that might minimise demand characteristics with honesty and researcher–participant rapport (see section 4).

4. This is another tricky one! You couldn't answer this only on the basis of your reading from section 4, 'alternatives to seeing psychology as a science', although this material is relevant. You couldn't even answer the question just from the issues covered in this chapter. You would need to think back to the chapters on the different approaches and branches of psychology (2 and 3). From this you can evaluate Kuhn's claim that psychology has no 'uniting paradigm'. You would want to refer to the big differences between the various approaches to psychology (psychodynamics, behaviourism, humanism, cognitivism, the physiological approach, etc.) and the ways in which they suggest that we should study human beings. From this you could argue about whether psychology today can be seen as having any 'uniting paradigm'. Then you could go on to explain how some psychologists have tried to make psychology into a science, while some have rejected the notion entirely, and say a bit about each of these positions (as in section 4). If this was an essay question, rather than an exam one, you would want to read up a bit more about Kuhn's points. These are covered in most introductory textbooks.

Section 6

Further reading and research

Some of the issues covered in this chapter are also mentioned in another book in the Crucial Study Text series, research methods and statistics, so you may want to read that too. There the issues are related to the research studies that you will carry out yourself as you progress through your psychology degree. Remember that some of the things you have learnt here will be useful for research methods modules, as well as for introductory modules and modules on the history of psychology.

Most introductory textbooks on psychology cover the issue of whether psychology is a science. You can get different perspectives and examples from each book. Two books that I found particularly useful are:

Malim, T. and Birch, A. (1998) *Introductory Psychology*. London: Macmillan Press.
Gross, R. (1995) *Themes, Issues and Debates in Psychology*. London: Hodder & Stoughton.

For a much more in-depth analysis of many of the issues covered in this chapter see:

Rosnow, R. L. and Rosenthal, R. (1997) *People Studying People: Artifacts and Ethics in Behavioural Research*. New York: W. H. Freeman.
Richards, G. (1996) *Putting Psychology in Its Place: An Introduction from a Critical Historical Perspective*. London: Routledge.

Gould's 'nation of morons' full article is in both these books:

Gross, R. (1999) *Key Studies in Psychology*. London: Hodder & Stoughton.
Banyard, P. and Grayson, A. (2000), *Introducing Psychological Research*. Basingstoke: Palgrave.

The latter book also contains Orne's original paper on demand characteristics and the articles by Kohlberg, Gilligan and Rosenthal.

For several perspectives on the qualitative/quantitative debate, see the following papers from *The Psychologist* magazine:

Morgan, M. (1996) 'Qualitative research: a package deal?' *The Psychologist,* January, 31–2.
Stevenson, C. and Cooper, N. (1997) 'Qualitative and quantitative research', *The Psychologist,* April, 159–60.
Sherrard, C. (1997) 'Never mind the bathwater, keep hold of the baby: qualitative research', *The Psychologist,* April, 161–2.
The Psychologist (1998) 'Quantitative vs. qualitative debate', November, 481–9.

You might also want to have a look at these references which were both mentioned in this chapter:

Pennebaker, J. W. (1997) *Opening Up: The Healing Power of Expressing Emotions.* London: Guilford Press.
Kitzinger, C., Coyle, A., Wilkinson, S. and Milton, M. (1998) 'Towards lesbian and gay psychology', *The Psychologist*, November, 529–33.

Chapter 5
Themes and debates in psychological theory

Chapter summary

We saw in Chapter 2 that the different approaches to psychology differ in both the assumptions they make about human beings and the methods they use to study them. Chapter 4 addressed current debates about the methods used, while this chapter considers issues around the assumptions underlying psychological theories. It covers four major debates about the nature of human beings that regularly come up in psychology.

The first three debates are the related questions of whether our behaviour is best explained by personal choice or by forces beyond our control (free will/determinism), at what level our behaviour can best be explained (reductionism), and whether our behaviour is best explained by biological or environmental factors (nature/nurture). The final debate is about how much psychology should take account of the ways that people in general understand human behaviour (common-sense understanding). The issue of whether psychology is a science (Chapter 4) comes into all these issues since determinism and reductionism are scientific assumptions, and psychology's desire for scientific status has distanced it from common-sense ideas about human behaviour.

Assessment targets

Target 1: Understanding free will/determinism
This chapter will help you to explore whether we freely choose to behave in certain ways or whether our behaviour is caused by influences beyond our control. You will see where the various approaches to psychology stand on this debate. Question 1 at the end of the chapter tests your grasp of this debate.

Target 2: Evaluating reductionist arguments and the mind–brain problem
Some psychologists argue that human functioning can best be explained by breaking it down into its constituent parts. This chapter will help you to understand some reductionist arguments and their strengths and weakness. It will also introduce the 'mind–brain' problem: whether consciousness/mental processes can be explained simply in terms of the functions of the brain. Question 2 at the end of the chapter tests your understanding of reductionism.

Target 3: Explaining the 'nature' and 'nurture' positions in psychology
Over the years, psychologists have hotly debated whether human functioning is best explained in terms of our innate biological make-up or external forces. This chapter will help you to understand this question of heredity versus environment, and the different positions psychologists have proposed. Question 3 at the end of the chapter tests your ability to evaluate nature and nurture positions.

Target 4: Exploring the relationship between psychology and 'common-sense' understanding
People in general have their own understandings about the way in which they, and other humans, function. This chapter will explain how psychology as a discipline relates to everyday people. Question 4 at the end of the chapter tests your knowledge of how psychology can relate to common-sense understanding.

How will you be assessed on this?

This chapter covers some key debates in psychology, which are often covered in introductory courses and in modules on the philosophy or history of psychology. You are likely to be given exam and essay questions asking you to evaluate each side of the debates (i.e. give their strengths and weaknesses). You may also be asked to summarise and evaluate the positions of key psychologists on these issues, so it is worth referring back to Chapter 2 throughout this chapter. The issue of psychology and common sense (section 4) is not covered in as many textbooks and psychology courses as the other debates mentioned here. However, it is a very important area in terms of justifying psychology's existence as a discipline and thinking about how it should relate to the general population. You are unlikely to be asked a specific question about this for an essay or exam unless it is covered in your course directly. However, this section will help you understand better psychology as it is today, and you can bring the ideas into answers to questions on the history of psychology (Chapter 1), pure and applied psychology (Chapter 3) and psychology as a science (Chapter 4).

Section 1

Free will and determinism

This section will cover the debate about whether human behaviour is determined by forces beyond our control or whether we freely choose to behave in the ways we do.

Why is this an issue in psychology?

CRUCIAL CONCEPT

Determinism is the belief that there are causes for every event that takes place. In psychology, it is the idea that all human behaviour is caused by influences beyond our control. Determinists believe that if we knew enough about a person we could explain all their actions and also predict what they would do in the future. Those who disagree with the deterministic view of human behaviour believe that, to some extent, we have 'free will' and can choose our actions.

CRUCIAL TIP

Before you read on, consider the debate for yourself. Think about some behaviours you carry out on a daily basis (e.g. eating breakfast, attending lectures, going out with friends). To what extent are these behaviours freely chosen or determined? What internal/external factors might they be determined by? Are you more inclined towards the free will or determinist position?

There are several reasons for the emphasis on the free will/determinism debate in psychology:

- As we saw in Chapter 1, psychology has strong roots in philosophy. Western philosophers have debated whether human behaviour is determined or freely chosen for centuries (certainly since Descartes in the 1600s who believed in free will). Therefore this inevitably became an important debate in psychology.

- As we saw in Chapter 4, most psychologists want to be seen as scientists. Determinism is one major assumption of science, since science tries to find causes for observed effects. Therefore many psychologists simply accept that all human behaviour is determined; our current behaviour is caused by what has happened to us previously and affects what will happen in the future, therefore we can explain and predict behaviour. However, we can question whether human behaviour is the same as the subjects studied by other sciences. We generally assume that people can make decisions and conscious choices in a way that chemicals or blood cells cannot.

- This debate has important implications for clinical psychology, which defines mental illness as loss of control, or free will, over behaviour. For example, a depressed person may be unable to prevent themselves from bursting into tears, or someone with 'Tourette's syndrome' may twitch or swear without consciously meaning to. This definition obviously implies that people without mental illnesses do have some kind of free will and control over their behaviour.

- As Gross (1999) points out, the debate is also vital in the area of criminal psychology due to notions of moral responsibility. Having 'lost control' (temporarily or permanently) is a legal defence. Psychologists may be involved in deciding whether someone has 'diminished responsibility'. If this defence is accepted in a murder case there will be no trial and the sentence of manslaughter will be passed. This has happened in some cases where women have killed while suffering from 'pre-menstrual syndrome' (Birch, 1993). The 'Yorkshire Ripper', Peter Sutcliffe, claimed that he suffered from paranoid schizophrenia because he heard the voice of God telling him to kill his victims. However, it was decided that this did not sufficiently impair his mental responsibility for his actions and he was given 20 life sentences. The notion of moral/legal responsibility is dependent on the idea that people are generally able to control their behaviour and have some kind of 'free will', otherwise how could we be held responsible for anything we do?

CRUCIAL TIP

Look back to the approaches to psychology we covered in Chapter 2. What would each of their positions be on this debate? Check Figure 2.6 to see whether you are right.

Determinism

In psychology, the psychoanalytic and behaviourist approaches are both deterministic. Both see 'free will' as an illusion, although they disagree about what factors cause behaviour. Freud (the founder of psychoanalysis) believed that human behaviour was determined by internal unconscious forces, whereas Skinner (a 'radical behaviourist') believed that it was determined by the environment.

For example, imagine that you love chocolate and you decide to eat a whole bar of it. You might think that you've made a free choice to do this, but neither Freud nor Skinner would agree with you. Freud might argue that you had unconscious sexual desires that you could not act upon, so you displaced that sexual energy into the more socially acceptable activity of eating chocolate (the defence mechanism of sublimation). Skinner might suggest that your love of chocolate was due to 'conditioning'. As a child, your grandparents didn't get to spend as much time as they wanted with you, so when they did spend time with you they gave you lots of chocolate and sweets to make up. You learned to associate sweets with the positive feeling of being loved by your grandparents, so now you eat chocolate to get that feeling again. (See Chapter 2 to remind yourself about Freud's defence mechanisms and the process of classical conditioning.)

Freud's 'psychic determinism' states that even seemingly random or irrational behaviours are determined by unconscious motivations. This includes mishaps and slips of the tongue, e.g. accidentally spilling coffee all over this book could mean that you've unconsciously had enough of reading about psychology! Despite Freud's therapeutic technique being called **'free** association', what it actually aims to do is to get at these unconscious causes of behaviour. The client may think they are randomly saying whatever comes into their head, but really there are reasons for all the things they say, which the psychoanalyst can interpret to reveal their unconscious thoughts and desires.

Skinner argued that our sense that we have free will is because some of the environmental causes of our behaviour are hidden. Causes are clear when there is a direct threat of punishment or possibility of reward (e.g. not committing a crime for fear of imprisonment, or buying a raffle ticket in the hope of winning a prize). In cases where the environmental causes are not so apparent it might seem that we are acting freely, but behaviour is still determined by things that have been rewarded or punished in the past (learnt responses like the example of the chocolate bar, or the conditioned fear of spiders discussed in Chapter 2). Radical behaviourists argue that we could predict all behaviours if we knew enough about people's histories of reinforcement.

Many evolutionary psychologists are also determinists because they argue that all human behaviour is explainable in terms of genetics and evolution (see Chapter 2). Determinist psychologists don't necessarily have to choose between internal (biological/psychic) or external (environmental) forces as an explanation for behaviour (see section 3 of this chapter). They may believe that human behaviour is determined by a combination of these factors. However, they do all share the belief that if psychologists could measure these things precisely enough we could accurately explain and predict all behaviour through the various factors acting on a person to cause their behaviour. Figure 5.1 summarises the arguments for and against the determinist position.

In addition to the arguments presented in Figure 5.1, another problem with determinism is that it means that we cannot praise or blame people for their behaviour (since it is not in their control); society would be a very different place if we totally accepted determinism.

Determinism doesn't fit very well with our common-sense understandings of ourselves (see section 4). Most of us certainly feel like we can make free decisions. As Stratton and Hayes (1999) point out, in practice, most psychologists see themselves as freely choosing to study the (deterministic) causes of behaviour! William James (1890) dealt with this by proposing that we should have one rule in science and another for everyday behaviour, since science could only progress by assuming determinism, but society needs a belief in free will for moral, legal, social and political matters.

James also proposed 'soft determinism' which argues that behaviour is only determined to a certain extent. It may constrain us to a few courses of behaviour, but we can freely choose between those courses (unless something is coercing us or compelling us). For example, we have to eat when we're hungry, but we can choose between a raw carrot and a chocolate bar (unless someone is holding a gun to our head, or we have an addiction to chocolate!). 'Hard' determinists argue that even that sense of conscious control that allows us to make such decisions is caused at some level, so we are not truly acting freely.

Arguments for determinism	Arguments against determinism
Determinism is compatible with the scientific method (one of the main assumptions of science). It means that behaviour can be explained and predicted. This would not be possible if we believed that people just make free choices, and then what would be the point of psychology?	Other sciences no longer assume determinism; they've had to build uncertainty/indeterminism into the basis of their theories (e.g. quantum physics, chaos theory). Since the subject of psychology (human behaviour) is even more unpredictable, we may well have to do the same.
Determinism suggests that we can control behaviour (since we can predict it). Therefore we should be able to improve the world. For example, Skinner's novel *Walden Two* (1948) argued that we could reach Utopia by positively reinforcing civilised behaviour in children.	It is unlikely that we could ever find out enough information about someone's current state to explain or predict their behaviour. It would take ages to find all the (internal and external) forces acting on them, by which point they would have moved on anyway.
Determinism has optimistic implications for criminal behaviour. If criminal acts were the result of free choice we should just punish criminals to get retribution. However, if criminals' behaviour is determined, we should be able to alter their behaviour (e.g. through psychoanalysis, genetic manipulation, or providing new learning experiences, depending on your brand of determinism).	Determinism is unfalsifiable. It can't be proved wrong even if it is wrong. If determinists can't find a cause for a behaviour they just assume they just haven't discovered it yet. If you ask a determinist to predict what you will do and then do something different to prove determinism wrong, they will say this is because their prediction added another cause to your behaviour and you would have behaved as they predicted if you hadn't known about the prediction.

Figure 5.1 Arguments for and against determinism

In Chapter 2 we saw that humanist psychologists believed that people have free will. Therefore they come the closest to completely rejecting determinism. Rogers saw humans as in charge of their own lives and personal growth, and therapy was about free human beings struggling to become even more free. However, humanists do accept that there are some constraints on behaviour, such as personal experiences that affect our sense of self-worth. Towards the end of his life, Rogers acknowledged that human behaviour was determined, and embraced a kind of 'soft determinism', the rather complex idea that people who were not psychologically healthy were forced to act in ways they would not choose to, while 'fully functioning' people could freely choose to behave in the way that was determined for them, and this was most fulfilling (Gross, 1999).

Free will

CRUCIAL TIP

Think about the definition of free will. If you think that you have some degree of free will over your behaviour, what do you mean by that? Can you see how a determinist might argue against your belief?

Free will is difficult to define. Valentine (1992) gives a list of what we could mean when we use the term:

- **Choice** – we have free will when we could have chosen to act differently in a situation. However, this is untestable because we could never go back in time to see whether we could truly have made a different choice.

- **Behaviour that is uncaused** – behaviour with no cause at all would be totally random behaviour. However, this is not what those who believe in free will mean by this, since when we choose to behave in a certain way it is not random. Gross (1999) states that if the opposite of 'free' is 'coerced or constrained', this would suggest that we are free when we are not coerced or constrained. This is the soft determinist view presented above, e.g. no one is holding a gun to our head and we are not being driven by internal addictions/compulsions.

- **Voluntary behaviour** – This is what most of us mean by free will, having control and being able to exert a voluntary choice over our behaviour. This is the opposite of involuntary behaviour, such as the reflex jerk response when the doctor hits our knee. Valentine (1992) gives the following study as evidence for the distinction between voluntary and involuntary behaviour.

CRUCIAL STUDY

Penfield (1947) stimulated the exposed brains of patients undergoing surgery. When he stimulated certain brain areas, the patient's limbs would move. However, even though these brain areas were the same ones normally involved in limb movement, the patients reported that the experience felt very different from initiating the movement themselves. This suggests that subjective experiences of limb movement cannot be explained just by stimulation of a certain brain area. Doing things voluntarily **feels different** to the same things happening involuntarily.

This study supports the argument that having free will is a vital part of our subjective experience of ourselves: we feel as if we are free. However, it does not prove that we actually are free. Behaviour that feels free may still be predetermined. Nisbett and Wilson (1977) carried out several studies displaying that people are unaware of the factors that determine their behaviour. For example, people were shown a table with several packets of stockings and asked to choose one. Nisbett and Wilson found that people were most likely to choose the packet to the far right of the table, regardless of which one it was, since this was the last one they looked at. Participants gave many explanations for why they chose the packet they did, but almost all denied that the positioning of the stockings was a factor. So it seems that none of Valentine's possible definitions of free will are completely adequate. Figure 5.2 summarises the arguments for and against the free will position.

Arguments for free will	Arguments against free will
Free will fits with our subjective experience; we feel that we make free choices to behave the way we do.	Valentine (1992) points out that subjective feelings are notoriously unreliable. However strongly we feel that we make free choices, this does not mean that we do.
If we didn't have free will we could have no concept of moral responsibility; no one could be held responsible for their actions.	It is extremely hard to define exactly what we mean by free will. There are several different possible definitions (see above) with different implications for the debate.
The free will position is optimistic, meaning that we can make choices about our behaviour.	Complete acceptance of free will would mean that our behaviours are not influenced by anything. This goes against common sense and psychology

Figure 5.2 Arguments for and against free will

Another problem is that if we completely accepted free will it would be hard to defend psychology. Unless some aspects of behaviour are determined, the scientific study of behaviour can't be justified. It could also be argued that psychology has already found many factors that determine behaviour, and these factors make it less and less likely that humans have free choice over their actions. Psychologists can't really accept the idea of totally free will because of the lack of adequate definitions and because psychologists must see human behaviour as to some extent explainable and predictable. Therefore the argument in psychology is more likely to be between 'hard' and 'soft' determinism. Malim and Birch (1998) conclude that it is more useful to see free will and hard determinism at extreme ends of a continuum. For each behaviour we should ask not whether it is free or determined, but where on the continuum it lies.

Section summary

This section has summarised the position of some major psychologists on the free will/determinism debate as well as presenting the strengths and weaknesses of both extremes of this argument and suggesting some possible alternatives (soft determinism and the idea of a continuum). We have also seen that the debate has important real-world applications to the areas of clinical and criminal psychology, considering the issue of personal responsibility.

Quick test

Provide a brief explanation of the extreme determinist and free will positions. Explain the strengths and weaknesses of each.

Section 2

Reductionism and the mind–brain problem

Linked to the determinist viewpoint is the idea of reductionism. Generally reductionist theories tend to be deterministic. Determinism proposes that behaviour is determined by factors we cannot freely control. Reductionism concerns the level on which these factors operate. It proposes that behaviour can be explained on one level of explanation. One type of reductionism is the notion that consciousness is just the functioning of the brain. The mind–brain debate in psychology relates to this idea.

Why is this an issue in psychology?

Reductionism is important in psychology because, like determinism and empiricism (discussed in Chapter 4), reductionism is a major assumption of science. For example, in biology organisms can be seen as made up of a system of organs, which can, in turn, be seen as being made up of complexes of cells (Gross, 1995). Most psychologists adopt the scientific method, so they embrace reductionism.

CRUCIAL CONCEPT

Reductionism is the argument that phenomena are nothing but their component or constituent parts, e.g. a kettle is nothing more than a plastic box, an element and some electrical components. To understand something we can 'reduce' it down to separate simpler parts, hence 'reductionism'. In psychology, reductionists believe that complex human behaviours can be explained by breaking them down into their constituent parts, with only one level of explanation being necessary for a full account of behaviour. For example, behaviourists explain behaviour in terms of learnt stimulus–response links, evolutionary psychologists explain it in terms of genes (see Chapter 2).

Different types of reductionism

Garnham (1991) defined reductionism as the idea that psychological explanations can be replaced by explanations in terms of brain functions, or even in terms of chemistry or physics. It could be seen that reductionism's ultimate aim is to explain all phenomena at the level of subatomic particles (electrons, protons, etc.), since this is the lowest level of explanation that we have (at the moment!). Figure 5.3 displays the hierarchy of different possible levels of explanation.

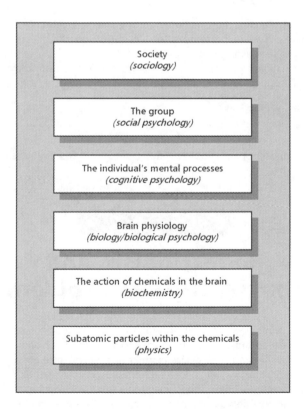

Figure 5.3 Hierarchy of levels of explanation of human behaviour
(and the areas that study them)

However, reductionism can more generally be understood as any attempt to explain phenomena at one level of this hierarchy in terms of levels below. It would be reductionist to explain an aspect of society in terms of the individuals who make up that society (e.g. explaining racism in terms of the prejudiced attitudes of individual people). It would also be reductionist to explain individual behaviour in terms of brain chemistry (e.g. explaining aggression in terms of someone's levels of testosterone).

Statton and Hayes' (1999) dictionary of psychology suggests using the example of telling a joke to show how a behaviour can be explained at different levels in this hierarchy, and how some levels of explanation might be more useful that others. Starting at the top of our hierarchy, we could explain telling a joke at the sociological level of the shared understandings necessary in a society for people to comprehend the joke (e.g. is it an 'Englishman, Irishman, Scotsman' joke, or a joke about typical gender behaviours?). Moving down the hierarchy, we could explain telling a joke in terms of its social function: getting a group of people to laugh and relax. We could explain it on the individual level in terms of the thought processes necessary for the joke-teller to produce the words and the listeners to comprehend them. We could explain the physiological processes necessary for the mouth to speak and the listeners to perceive the sounds, or we could explain the chemical state in the brain and body before, during and after the telling of the joke.

--- CRUCIAL TIP ---

To help you understand reductionism better, try going through these levels of explanation with your own example, e.g. shaking hands with a friend, having a drink in the pub, going to a movie.

So what is the most useful level of explanation? This really depends on the question being asked. Psychology usually asks two types of questions about behaviour: how and why. Different levels of explanation may be appropriate for each type of question. The question 'why do people tell jokes?' is probably most suitably answered on the social psychological level, whereas the question 'how do people tell jokes?' is probably best answered at a lower level in terms of how people produce and understand language. It seems nonsensical to explain a human behaviour such as joke-telling at the lowest level of subatomic particles. This is the argument against the most extreme version of reductionism that attempts to explain everything at the lowest level possible.

Two major types of reductionism are prevalent in psychology which involve explaining human behaviour at a simpler level (Malim and Birch, 1998):

- **Physiological reductionism** is the view that psychological explanations can be replaced by physiological explanations, since human beings are biological organisms. The most common explanations given are the functions of the brain and/or of human genes. An example of such reductionism is recent research into mental disorders like schizophrenia and depression that has found them to have a physiological basis. Schizophrenia has been explained as a malfunction of brain chemistry (too much dopamine). This explanation seems useful because it is simple and also suggests a successful treatment (drugs that reduce dopamine). However, there are problems with this perspective of schizophrenia. First, showing that schizophrenics have too much dopamine does not show whether this is the cause of schizophrenia or an effect of it. It could be that schizophrenia is caused by environmental factors that increase levels of dopamine in the brain, and therefore could be addressed by altering the environment rather than giving people drugs. Also the dopamine theory does not explain why, in Britain, Afro-Caribbean people are around four times more likely to be diagnosed schizophrenic than white people, and why these levels vary across cultures (Banyard, 1996).

- **Biological reductionism** attempts to explain human behaviour in terms of less complex animals. This is the view held by many evolutionary psychologists and sociobiologists (see Chapter 2). Examples include Lorenz, who put forward a theory of human aggression based on his observations of different animal behaviours, and

E.O. Wilson, who claimed that human behaviours, such as mating, could be explained in the same ways as those of animals. The difficulty with this is that it is problematic to make comparisons between humans and other animals living today. Humans and other primates may have evolved from the same starting point, but they then went along different lines. They have evolved differently in terms of physiology and behaviour, so it may not be particularly helpful to make comparisons between them. Biological reductionism also neglects the importance of culture in human behaviour (see section 3 of this chapter).

Other approaches to psychology are also reductionist. Behaviourism reduces behaviour to combinations of stimulus–response associations, and psychoanalysis reduces it to unconscious desires and fears. Traditional cognitive psychology has been described as 'machine reductionist' (Malim and Birch, 1998) since it uses computer models to explain some aspects of human behaviour. Machine reductionism has been accused of overlooking the many differences between humans and computers (see Chapter 2). More recent 'connectionist' cognitive psychology is not machine reductionist, since it acknowledges these problems with the computer model. Connectionism models mental processes on the brain, so it might seem, at face value, to be guilty of physiological reductionism. However, connectionists point out that it isn't attempting to find a true neural basis of cognition. Rather it is just using a neural 'model' to try to understand how mental processes work. Therefore connectionist cognitive psychology is interested in explanations at the level of mental processes and is not concerned with 'lower' levels. In this sense, it could also be said to be reductionist, since it is still mostly interested in one level of explanation.

Gestalt psychology (Chapter 1) was non-reductionist in its view that 'the whole is greater than the sum of its parts'. Much social psychology would also suggest a non-reductionist view of the world since social psychologists have found that group behaviour cannot always be explained by understanding the individuals who make up a group. Moscovici and Zavalloni (1969) found that people in groups tend to make decisions that are more extreme than the average of the group member's initial positions, so a discussion between a group of people who slightly disagree with fox hunting is likely to produce a group decision that strongly opposes fox hunting.

Figure 5.4 below summarises the main arguments for and against reductionism in general.

Arguments for reductionism	Arguments against reductionism
Reductionism is part of the scientific approach, so fits in with psychology's aim to be a science. Behaviour explained in reductionist ways can be described concretely.	The extreme reductionist perspective would leave no need for psychology, since everything could be explained at the level of physics (see joke example from earlier for how nonsensical this can be).
Some psychological questions are best answered at lower levels – 'how' questions.	Some psychological questions are not well answered at lower levels, – 'why' questions.
Reductionism gives simple, concise explanations for psychological phenomena.	Reductionist arguments overlook other levels of explanation. This produces limited understanding of phenomena.
Reductionism can suggest successful interventions (see earlier example of dopamine and schizophrenia).	Reductionism doesn't take account of 'emergent properties'. These are characteristics that appear in combinations of elements that couldn't be predicted from the individual elements. For example, people in groups and crowds behave differently to the way they do as individuals. Reductionism would not predict this.
	Reductionist explanations can be sought for particular reasons or political purposes. For example, a government that wants to avoid dealing with crime can explain it at a biological level (it's in the genes) rather than a social one (the result of deprivation or poor education).

Figure 5.4 Arguments for and against reductionism

The mind–brain debate

Another issue that relates to reductionism is the mind–brain debate. Like the free will/determinism debate, this originates in philosophy, particularly the ideas of Descartes, where it was known as the mind–body problem (see Chapter 1). Today it is an issue hotly debated by psychologists and biologists. The mind–brain question is whether consciousness (or the mind) can be completely explained by the functions of the brain, or whether there is more to it than this. I will provide a brief summary here of reductionist and non-reductionist theories of the mind–brain relationship, but you should look at Gross's books for a more detailed explanation of all the different perspectives beyond psychology. This debate also links into the question of whether psychology should study mental processes (see Chapter 2), and whether machines could ever be conscious (see Gross and McIlveen, 1999, and Searle, 1980).

Few psychologists would argue that more than the physical brain is involved in human behaviour, since this seems to imply something beyond scientific understanding (e.g. a soul or spirit, something supernatural). Most psychologists are materialists.

CRUCIAL CONCEPT

Materialism is the belief that nothing exists apart from the material world; materialist psychologists generally agree that consciousness (the mind) is a function of the brain. Mental processes can be identified with purely physical processes in the central nervous system, and human beings are just complicated physiological organisms, no more than that.

What psychologists disagree on is whether everything can be adequately explained at the level of the physical brain. Physiological reductionist materialists attempt to reduce all human behaviour to the level of the brain. For example, Crick (1994) said: 'You, your joys and your sorrows, your memories and your ambitions, your sense of personality and free will, are in fact no more than the behaviour of a vast assembly of nerve cells and their associated molecules' (quoted in Gross, 1995, p. 312). This view implies that whenever a certain mind state occurs, a certain brain state occurs; the same brain state in each person leads to the same conscious experience. This has been disputed by non-reductionist psychologists, who have shown that two people can use different brain mechanisms for the same behaviour, such as reading (Broadbent, 1981). The brain can perform the same task in several different ways. Studies on brain-damaged patients have found that other areas of the brain sometimes compensate for the functions that have been lost.

This suggests that consciousness can only be understood by studying the whole brain, rather than the individual areas that make it up. Consciousness is an 'emergent property' of the brain, because it could not be predicted from simply analysing the areas that make up the whole system (see Figure 5.4); consciousness is a property of the interactions between the various parts of it. Each person has a unique consciousness (or mind) because their individual neurons and the connections between them are wired up in different ways.

So although most psychologists are materialists, some of them are reductionists and some of them are not. Non-reductionist materialists believe that there are two different languages (or levels of description) in psychology, one for the mind and one for the brain. The brain is necessarily involved in everything we do, but may not always be useful in the explanation of our behaviour. Going back to the example of telling a joke from earlier, we saw that this could be explained at the level of neurons firing, but that a more useful description would be at a higher level. We can describe and explain our mental processes (mind) without having to 'bring the brain into it' (Gross and McIlveen, 1999).

Section summary

We have seen that reductionism tries to explain psychological phenomena at lower levels of explanation. This could be a threat to psychology if it were possible to explain all human behaviour at the level of biology (or even chemistry or physics). Physiological reductionists have attempted to explain all behaviour at the level of the brain; however, there have been several problems with this. This links in with the mind–brain debate, where we have seen that it is useful to have a language of the mind, as well as one of the brain.

Quick test

Describe the two main types of reductionism and give examples of each one. What are the main problems with these perspectives?

Section 3

The nature–nurture debate

One of the most recurrent and heated issues in psychology is the nature–nurture (or heredity–environment) debate. This follows from the previous debates we have covered, because those on both sides of this argument believe that behaviour is determined, though they differ over whether they think it is determined by our genetic make-up (the nature, heredity or nativist position) or environmental forces (the nurture, environment or empiricist position). Extremes of both these positions are reductionist, since they explain all behaviour at one level of explanation.

As we will see in this section, most psychologists now accept that **both** heredity and the environment are necessary for human existence and influence our behaviour, and that the either/or nature/nurture question is oversimplified. Therefore the question has shifted to considering to what extent nature or nurture affects our behaviour and how they interact.

Why is this an issue in psychology?

Like the free will/determinism debate, this issue dates back to the early western philosophers, specifically Descartes (a nativist) and Locke (an empiricist) in the 1600s.

CRUCIAL CONCEPT

Nativists come from the nature/heredity side of the debate. They believe that babies carry an inborn (innate) blueprint that will determine their character and behaviour. Some behaviours will be present from birth, while others will emerge during development on a pre-programmed time schedule as children mature. Today, nativists believe that the blueprint is inherited through genetic transmission. Individual differences between people are explained by their genotypes (the set of genes that they possess). The environment the person is in has little impact on their development, so there is little possibility that they can change from their predetermined course.

CRUCIAL CONCEPT

Empiricists come from the nurture/environment side of the debate. They believe that newborn children are blank slates (tabulae rasae), whose behaviour and character is shaped by their environment. As the child grows, behaviours are acquired as a result of experiences, particularly learning. Empiricism allows the possibility of change. Within their physical limitations and given the right environment, anyone can become anything.

CRUCIAL TIP

Note that this definition of 'empiricism' is different to the one given in the previous chapter. In the context of methods, empiricism means accurate measurement; in the context of nativism vs. empiricism it means belief in the importance of nurture. The two uses of the term can be confusing, so make sure you always check the context it is being used in.

Nativist and empiricist positions in psychology

Examples of extreme nativist positions in psychology include those of the Gestalt psychologists (see Chapter 1), who believed that the perceptual system was innate, and the experience of perceiving things in our environment had little impact on it. Chomsky's cognitive theory of language was also nativist (see Chapter 2). Chomsky proposed that we are born with a brain mechanism he called the 'language acquisition device' (LAD). This contains most of the necessary rules about the structure of language which we use progressively as we mature and develop language skills. This view is supported by findings that children everywhere acquire language in a short space of time, at approximately the same age and in the same sequence (Lenneberg, 1967).

The main extreme empiricists in psychology were the behaviourists (see Chapters 1 and 2). Skinner argued that behaviour was entirely learnt through a process of shaping and reinforcement. For example, his theory of language contrasts directly with Chomsky's (see Figure 5.5).

Watson sets out the extreme empiricist view of the behaviourists like this:

> Give me a dozen healthy infants, well-formed, and my own specified world to bring them up in and I'll guarantee to take any one at random and train him to become any type of specialist I might select – a doctor, lawyer, artist, merchant-chief and, yes, even into beggar-man and thief, regardless of his talents, penchants, abilities, vocations and race of his ancestors.
>
> (Watson, 1930, quoted in Furnham, 2001)

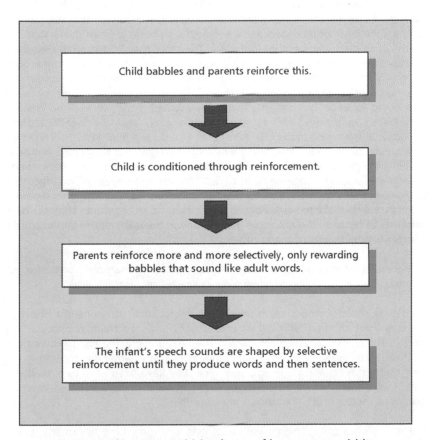

Figure 5.5 Skinner's empiricist theory of language acquisition

The interactionist perspective

Few psychologists today would put forward an extreme nativist or empiricist view, since almost all features of human beings have been found to have both genetic and environmental components. Going back to language, Skinner's empiricist view was found to be flawed because evidence suggests that parents very rarely correct bad grammar or reward proper use of grammar in their children, and yet children still manage to learn grammatical rules. Chomsky's LAD was also found to be problematic because it ignores the fact that parents often do modify their language to help children understand (child-directed speech or 'motherese'), and the LAD does not explain how children learn the social function of language. Current language acquisition theories suggest an interaction between inherited traits and experience of the environment.

CRUCIAL CONCEPT

Interactionists believe that inherited characteristics interact with environmental factors to produce human behaviour and characteristics. Most psychologists today are interactionists.

Now psychologists accept that nature and nurture interact to produce behaviour, the next questions they can ask are:

- To what extent is a behaviour determined by each factor?
- How does the environment interact with the biological factors?

The first question is nearly as problematic as the question of whether behaviour is determined entirely by nature of nurture. Psychologists have tried to find out how much of a characteristic like intelligence is inherited and how much is due to the environment. However, genes do not map simply onto behaviours in such a way that we can find one gene for, say, violence or intelligence. Each individual inherits a set of genes that combine to determine, to some degree, their potential. There are over 70 trillion different possible combinations of genes (Malim and Birch, 1998). Also, genes can't determine behaviour directly, only via the environment, and the environment can't affect behaviour directly, only through the genetic make-up of the individual. For example, a person might be genetically predisposed to violence, but this might not be revealed if they were in an environment where violence simply wasn't allowed (e.g. a culture which strongly discouraged violence, such as Japan or the Amish in the US). Alternatively, a person might have been brought up in a very violent community, developing a violent character, but they could not be violent themselves because of a genetic disorder that gave them a very tiny frame and weak physique. Steve Jones (1993) states that genetic factors and environmental factors are so closely blended that it is impossible to tease them apart. It is like trying to separate cake ingredients once the cake has been baked. From this we can conclude that it is better for psychologists to focus on the nature of the interaction between nature and nurture and in what ways changes in one of them influence the other.

To see how this interactionism works, let's look at some examples: one of a physical characteristic (height) and one psychological characteristic (intelligence).

There is a clear genetic component in physical characteristics such as height. Short parents usually have short children, and tall parents usually have tall children because height is inherited in the child's genotype. However, the environment the child grows up in can disrupt this. This includes the environment while they are developing in the womb (e.g. the mother's diet, smoking and drinking), and once they have been born (e.g. their diet and posture). This explains why the average height of people has increased over time as environmental factors such as nutrition have improved.

If there are such strong environmental effects on something as clearly genetically determined as height, it is likely that this will also be the case for psychological characteristics and behaviours. There has been a great deal of psychological research into how heredity affects intelligence. Francis Galton, Charles Darwin's cousin, proposed that intelligence was inherited in the 1800s. His evidence was that many eminent men (judges, politicians, etc.) also had eminent relatives. Of course this doesn't take account of the similar environments that such people come from. In Chapter 1 we saw that twins have been studied a great deal to see whether characteristics are inherited. Figure 5.6 summarises some of the main evidence in this field.

The correlation between the IQ scores of monozygotic (genetically identical) twins brought up together was 0.86. For dizygotic (genetically non-identical) twins brought up together it was 0.60.

The correlation between the IQ scores of adopted monozygotic twins who were brought up in different homes was 0.72.

The correlation between the IQs of biologically related siblings (sisters and brothers) brought up together was 0.47. If they were adopted and brought up in different homes it was 0.24.

For adopted siblings who were not actually biologically related to each other, the correlation between IQ scores was 0.31.

Figure 5.6 Intelligence quotient (IQ) correlations in twins and siblings (Bouchard and McGuire, 1981)

CRUCIAL TIP

A **correlation** tells us how much two things are related. A score of 1 means they are completely related, and 0 means they are not related at all.

These findings suggest that there is some genetic component to intelligence (as measured by IQ scores) because genetically identical twins had more related IQs than those who were not genetically identical. This is also supported by findings that adopted children's IQs are more similar to those of their biological parents than those of their adopted parents.

However, if IQ was completely inherited, we would expect monozygotic twins to have a correlation of 1, since they share exactly the same genes. The fact that the correlation is less than 1 suggests that the environment plays some role, as does the finding that twins and siblings have less correlated IQs when they are brought up apart than when they are brought up together. Evidence that the environment affects intelligence also comes from the finding that children who are not genetically related but are brought up in the same house have correlated IQs, and the fact that dizygotic twins have more related IQs than ordinary siblings. Both these groups share 50 per cent of their genes, so we would expect their IQs to correlate the same amount if IQ was inherited. The fact the correlation is lower for ordinary siblings is because twins are likely to share a more similar environment within the home, since they are the same age. Scarr and Weinberg (1976) also found that children from a deprived African-American neighbourhood who were adopted by a middle-class white family scored more highly on IQ tests than those who remained in the neighbourhood.

Scarr (1992) also argues that people are not simply influenced **by** their environment, but also have an influence back **on** the environment, helping to shape and create their own experiences. In other words, the environment and the individual interact. This is a constructionist view (see Chapter 2). Examples of this include the finding, in aggression research, that aggressive children tend to elicit hostile responses from other children, which in turn makes them more aggressive (Rutter and Rutter, 1993). In gender research, the biological sex of a child has been found to influence the way that adults react to it, in turn influencing how the child behaves. Will et al. (1976) gave young mothers a baby (not their own) to play with and observed their behaviour. The same baby was either dressed in pink and given a girl's name, or dressed in blue and given a boy's name. The mothers smiled at the 'girl' more, were more likely to give them a doll to play with, and described them as being 'sweet' and having a 'soft cry'.

Ruble (1988) suggests how nature and nurture factors might interact in complex ways to produce different behaviours in the two genders. Genetic factors influence prenatal hormone levels and other biological factors, creating predispositions in children towards masculine or feminine characteristics. Then, from the moment of birth, gender-stereotyped expectations exert shaping influences on children's behaviours. Small sex differences may be exacerbated by parents' willingness to conform to stereotypes (e.g. boys may be born more active, and parents may play more roughly with them, making them even more active and aggressive). By the age of three, children themselves start trying to understand rules about gender behaviour, possibly because an inbuilt cognitive mechanism kicks in at this age. Their internal motivations to act appropriately are added to external pressures for boys and girls to behave in certain ways. The gender-stereotyped models available in our culture are then integrated into children's emerging rule-systems and act as guidelines for behaviour.

Going back to Steve Jones' analogy of separating out genetic and environmental influences being like separating the ingredients once a cake is baked, Ruble's example of gender illustrates this well. Like a cake, the making of a person is a process involving constant mixing together different ingredients (nature and nurture). Just as you could not understand what a cake would end up looking/tasting like from analysing the whole eggs, flour, etc. you could not predict what a person will become from simply analysing their childhood environment or strands of their DNA (the molecules that contain our genes).

The tendency towards 'nature' explanations

It seems from the above that it is accepted that genetics and the environment interact in shaping human behaviour. Some people suggest that our genes provide the upper and lower limits to behaviour and the environment determines whereabouts we fall between those limits. However, recent genetics research suggests that our genes do not place such fixed limits on our behaviour, and that there is even flexibility in some genetic characteristics (Malim and Birch, 1998).

Given all this, it is strange that much popular psychology (television documentaries, self-help books, etc.) only presents the 'nurture' side of the argument. I have seen so many TV programmes talking about genes for violence or serial killing. Many 'pop' psychology books propose that men and women have evolved to behave in different ways (see Figure 5.7), or that personality characteristics are genetically determined.

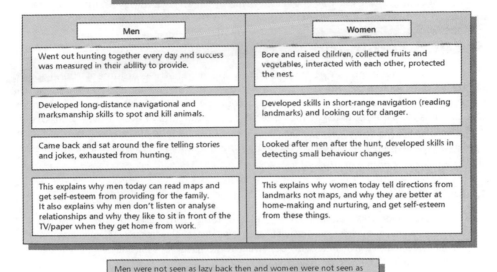

In prehistoric times, men and women lived happily together in harmony, because they had clear, accepted roles for which they evolved specialised skills. This lasted hundreds of thousands of years.

Men	Women
Went out hunting together every day and success was measured in their ability to provide.	Bore and raised children, collected fruits and vegetables, interacted with each other, protected the nest.
Developed long-distance navigational and marksmanship skills to spot and kill animals.	Developed skills in short-range navigation (reading landmarks) and looking out for danger.
Came back and sat around the fire telling stories and jokes, exhausted from hunting.	Looked after men after the hunt, developed skills in detecting small behaviour changes.
This explains why men today can read maps and get self-esteem from providing for the family. It also explains why men don't listen or analyse relationships and why they like to sit in front of the TV/paper when they get home from work.	This explains why women today tell directions from landmarks not maps, and why they are better at home-making and nurturing, and get self-esteem from these things.

Men were not seen as lazy back then and women were not seen as oppressed by men. This is how gender behaviour evolved and explains the problems between the genders today.

Figure 5.7 Ideas from the pop psychology book *Why Men Don't Listen and Women Can't Read Maps* (Pease and Pease, 1999)

CRUCIAL TIP

Look out for TV documentaries and 'popular psychology' books on psychological matters. Try to read them keeping in mind the ideas put forward in this chapter. Do you think the producers put across more of the 'nature' side of the argument and less of the 'nurture'? If so, why might they do this? What impact does it have on how non-psychologist viewers/readers understand human behaviour? Try this now for the example given in Figure 5.7. You could also refer back to the criticisms of evolutionary psychology in section 4 of Chapter2.

A possible reason for this popular focus on genetic and biological explanations of behaviour is that they are simpler than considering all the complex interactions between inherited and environmental factors. Also these explanations can let us off the hook as a society. There is nothing that we, or the government, can do about poverty, crime or sexism if it is all the result of evolution and biology and therefore unchangeable.

Chapter 4 showed how genetic theories of intelligence have been used to claim that racial difference are genetic, and how this has fuelled racism and inequality. Genetic theories are often used as a chance to excuse injustice (Byrne, 1994). If a group is seen as genetically different it may be more acceptable to treat them differently, or even to prevent them from reproducing. 'Eugenicists' believe that human society can be improved by 'good breeding'. In the 1920s and 1930s, such arguments resulted in the US restricting immigration of 'undesirable' races (see Chapter 4) and sterilising people in prisons and psychiatric units, as well as the Nazis exterminating Jews, homosexuals and other 'undesirable' people in the gas chambers.

Today, the identification of a 'gay gene' (really the isolation of a segment of a chromosome containing several hundred genes, which may be linked to male homosexuality) has important social and political implications (LeVay and Hamer, 1994). It could be used against gay people who have fought for their right to choose their sexual preference, although it could also be used to support the argument that homosexuality is 'natural'.

The next section explores further the relationship between psychology and the way people in general understand human behaviour (including the authors of pop psychology!).

Section summary

Two extreme reductionist views in psychology are the 'nature' argument (behaviour is determined by genetics) and the 'nurture' argument (behaviour is determined by the environment). We have seen that few psychologists today hold these extreme positions, and that it is problematic to ask 'which one' (nature or nurture) or even 'how much' of each aspect explains a behaviour. It is better to examine how genetic and environmental factors interact, and we have seen some possible interactionst explanations of intelligence and gender.

Quick test

1. Read back over this section, then make a table summarising the strengths and weaknesses of the extreme nativist and empiricist arguments. Think about what makes these views attractive or unattractive to people in general, as well as the evidence against them from psychology.
2. Give an 'interactionist' explanation of one aspect of human behaviour, showing how genetics and the environment might come together to cause it.

Section 4

Psychology and common sense

Psychology is different from many other sciences because it involves studying humans and their behaviour. Humans are unique among animals in their ability to consider their own existence and to come up with explanations for the behaviour of themselves and others that help them to function on a daily basis. This section explains some of the problems involved for psychology in studying things that people already have some understanding of. This will help you to consider how psychology should position itself in relation to everyday 'common-sense' understandings of human behaviour.

Why is this an issue in psychology?

--- CRUCIAL CONCEPT ---

Common-sense understanding means the way that people in general make sense of the world and understand human behaviour. Some psychologists have also called this 'lay psychology', 'everyday psychology' or 'folk psychology', meaning the psychology of 'ordinary' people, as opposed to professional or academic psychologists.

Psychologists need to think about common-sense understanding of the world for three main reasons:

- It is an interesting area of psychological study in its own right.
- It might threaten psychology as a discipline.
- If psychology wants to be relevant to lay people (non-psychologists), it needs to consider (and perhaps build on) their existing understandings.

I will not spend much time on the first of these reasons, but you can read up about the area of 'attribution theory' in social psychology, which has investigated how people understand the world they live in and make attributions about it (explaining why things happened in the way they did – see Gross, 1995). Here we will briefly examine the other two reasons for psychology needing to take account of common-sense understanding.

Common-sense understanding – a threat to psychology?

In a way we are all psychologists. We are all involved in explaining our own behaviour and that of other people – this is necessary in order for us to be able to function in the world. When we have an argument with a close friend, we often spend a lot of time afterwards trying to explain why we both reacted in the way we did. When we buy someone a present, we try to predict what that person would like based on what we know about their character and past behaviour. When we give a presentation at work or college, we try to understand how the audience will comprehend and react to what we are saying. Jones and Elcock (2001) point out that autistic people (who lack this ability to 'psychologise') find such social interactions very difficult.

But if we were all perfect psychologists, there would be no need for the discipline of psychology at all. Probably for this reason, several books on psychology aimed at lay people start off with long questionnaires just to prove how little the reader really knows about human behaviour! Colman (1999) and Furnham (2001) both include such questionnaires; you might find it interesting to have a go yourself.

What these questionnaires attempt to prove is that people's common-sense understanding of human behaviour is not as good as that of academic psychology. This is because academic psychology studies things scientifically and rigorously, coming up with objective evidence about behaviour. Common-sense understanding, on the other hand, is often inaccurate because it is:

- based on lack of knowledge;
- subjective (based on our own personal opinion);
- unreliable (because it varies from person to person);
- frequently biased (because people often hold prejudiced beliefs).

Chapter 4 shows that academic psychological theories have also been accused of being biased in the past, but at least psychological evidence can be checked and reanalysed to reveal such biases in a way that common-sense understanding cannot.

The psychologist Hans Eysenck (1957) maintained that 'the basis of common-sense is prejudice and political ideology'. Furnham (2001), Shermer (1997) and Hyman (1977) all present convincing evidence that common-sense understanding is flawed since it is often based on superstition and credulity. This explains why people believe in 'pseudo-sciences' such as astrology and graphology (handwriting analysis), for which there is no scientific evidence.

Psychologists have also displayed the inadequacies of common-sense understanding by pointing out that it frequently contradicts itself. Think of well-known sayings such as 'look before you leap' and 'he who hesitates is lost', or 'too many cooks spoil the broth' and 'many hands make light work'. Some psychologists have studied people's understandings and predictions about human behaviour and found these to be faulty. For example, Nisbett and Wilson (1977) presented people with passages of text from a harrowing book. Some of them were given the entire passage, while others were given the passage with a part missing. Participants who received the passage with a part missing reported that the text would have been more harrowing if they had read the whole passage. However, the researchers found that the difference between subjects who received the whole text and those who didn't was not nearly as great as the participants predicted. As we saw earlier, Nisbett and Wilson's studies also contradict the idea that we make free choices, which is a fundamental aspect of most people's common-sense conception of human behaviour.

It is evident that common-sense understanding is not particularly accurate, and that it is often subjective and unreliable. In the applied area of occupational psychology (see Chapter 3), lay people involved in job interviews have been found to hold an alarming number of irrational biases which seriously undermine the validity and reliability of the selection procedure. Anderson and Shackleton (1993) identified twelve major dysfunctions repeatedly found in studies in several countries. These included interviewers forming impressions of the candidate in the first few minutes and only seeking to confirm their perceptions, interviewers selecting candidates similar to themselves in biographical background, personality and attitudes, and the fundamental attribution error, where interviewers incorrectly attributed the cause of candidate behaviour to their personality rather than to the situational constraints and demands (like the stressful situation of the interview).

The relationship between psychology and common-sense understanding

Because of these problems with common-sense understanding, many psychologists have not really taken account of the way that people in general think about the issues they study. However, Clarke (1987) argues that psychology's ignorance of common-sense under-standing is a problem, because psychology seeks to replace common-sense knowledge with something completely separate, rather than extending and enriching it. Lay people are forced to discard academic psychology in favour of their own common-sense beliefs, which are far too important for them to reject. Clarke explains this using a diagram, which I have adapted in Figure 5.8 and consider in detail below.

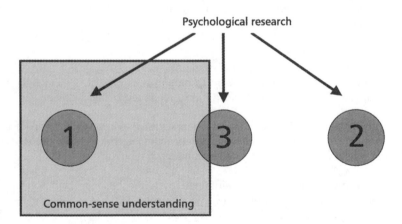

Figure 5.8 Psychological research in relation to common-sense understanding

1. Redundant findings

One of the most prevalent objections to psychology on the part of lay people is that the findings are not surprising because they already knew them. Ignorance of common-sense understanding can lead to the complaint that psychological research is pointless because it only discovers the obvious. Houston (1983) states that 'a great many of psychology's basic principles are self-evident. One gets the uneasy feeling that we have been dealing with the obvious and did not know it.' He constructed 21 multiple-choice questions about various memory and learning phenomena and found that lay people answered 16 of the items more accurately than would be expected by chance. For example, most people knew that the best way to remember a word is to use deep-level processing (to think about its meaning rather than what it looks or sounds like).

2. Unusable findings

Another common objection to psychological research is that the findings are unusable. This could be because they contradict very strongly held common-sense opinions and therefore threaten people, for example Milgram's finding that most people would give high electric shocks to another person simply because a scientist told them to. Alternatively, findings could simply be irrelevant because they seem trivial or because they answer questions that lay people were not interested in. Either way, any findings are unlikely to be applied, and are therefore unusable. In its aim to be scientific, psychology may have limited its areas of study to those that are less interesting to lay people, and made itself inaccessible to those without a great deal of relevant training.

CRUCIAL TIP

Look back at the discussion of pure and applied psychology in Chapter 3. Think about how these issues might affect pure psychology and applied psychology. Pure psychologists might be concerned that people wouldn't understand their theories/findings or be interested in them. Applied psychologists might be more concerned that people wouldn't use their theories/findings in the workplace, school, hospital, etc.

---

3. Helpful findings (that build on common sense)

It seems that psychology must take some account of common sense if it is to be credible, non-threatening, new, interesting and usable. Psychology that built on existing common-sense understanding would be much more likely to be applied and would not simply tell people what they already knew.

Academic psychology and common-sense understanding do influence each other. Ideas from psychology like IQ and ego have become part of everyday language. Also, the concerns of ordinary people become hot topics in psychology (e.g. obedience after the Holocaust, and gambling after the introduction of the National Lottery). We shouldn't forget that psychologists come from planet earth just like everyone else – outside the psychology lab most of them rely on common-sense understanding to function in the world too! This is bound to have some impact on their work. So, perhaps psychologists should be more open to a dialogue with common-sense understanding.

Jones and Elcock (2001) argue that some psychological theories have been incorporated into common-sense understanding, but these often tend to be the least rigorous and scientific approaches such as psychoanalysis, since these address people's everyday concerns in a way that most academic psychology does not (see Chapter 2). There is a danger, if psychologists ignore common-sense understanding, that people will turn to popular psychology instead, which does address issues of concern and explains them in ways that lay people can understand, engaging with fashionable and interesting topics (e.g. relationships, crime, the interpretation of dreams and body language).

As we saw in the previous section, 'pop' psychology often relies on reductionist and oversimplified explanations for complex human behaviour, for example the idea that all gender differences are due to evolution, rather than being a complex interaction between genetics and cultural gender-roles. Other popular explanations of human behaviour include the notions that media violence causes child crime, or that a brain dysfunction makes people into serial killers. There are really many complex reasons why a child would commit an act of violence or a person would become a murderer. Unfounded claims about racial or gender differences or genetic bases of behaviours may be damaging and reinforce prejudice (Jones and Elcock, 2001). If psychology doesn't address the concerns of everyday people in a way they can easily understand it seems likely that they will continue to turn to this less rigorous and critical brand of 'pseudo-psychology' which fills the existing gap between academic psychology and everyday people.

People seem to be growing more and more interested in human behaviour, if television programmes are anything to go on (for example *Big Brother* on Channel 4, *The Human Zoo* on ITV1 or *The Experiment* on BBC1). If there is a receptive audience then perhaps this is the time for academic psychology to present its theories and findings, retaining their complexity and rigour, but also putting them across in understandable accessible language, taking account of people's common-sense understanding and dealing with issues that are important to them.

Section summary

In this section we have addressed the relationship between psychology and common-sense understanding of human behaviour. We have seen that common-sense understanding is often flawed, but that it is also all ordinary people have to go on because they don't feel that academic psychology speaks to them. Psychological findings often seem obvious, irrelevant or threatening to people, so they turn to their own common sense, or 'pop' psychology. In the last section we looked at how psychology could build on common-sense understanding rather than rejecting it.

Quick test

In what ways is academic psychology superior to common-sense understandings of human behaviour? Why doesn't this mean that psychologists can just ignore common sense?

Section 5

End of chapter assessment

Questions

These questions relate to the four assessment targets set at the beginning of this chapter. If you can answer them effectively you are in a good position to get good credit in assessments or examinations.

1. What are the strengths and weaknesses of the determinist position in psychology?
2. Describe two reductionist theories in psychology. What are the problems with these?
3. How might human aggression be explained by a nativist, an empiricist and an interactionist?
4. Should psychologists take account of 'everyday psychology'?

Answers

1. This is a fairly straightforward question. If it was a short-answer question in an exam, you could just give bullet points of the strengths and weaknesses drawing on Figure 5.1 and also the issues about mental illness and personal responsibility for crimes covered at the start of this section.

   If this was an essay question, you would want to begin with more of an explanation of the background of the debate about determinism. You could then outline the strengths and weaknesses of determinism, giving examples to illustrate these, and then go on to outline the alternatives to determinism and any problems with these (complete free will and the 'soft determinist' position), coming to a conclusion about the most useful perspective in psychology.

2. For this question, you could pick any two of the reductionist theories we covered: physiological reductionist theories, biological reductionist theories, behaviourism, psychoanalysis or cognitive psychology, which is machine reductionist. It would probably be worth picking at least one of the first two of these though, because we covered those in more depth.

For a short-answer exam question, you should just take each of the theories you have chosen in turn, describe briefly how they are reductionist and what the drawbacks of this are. For a longer essay question, you could explain the theories in more detail, and draw some more general conclusions about the problems with reductionist theories. Some of the material from section 3 (nature–nurture) might also be helpful here because you could explain why it is problematic to reduce human behaviour to just biology or just the environment.

3. This question is asking you to take the ideas covered in section 3 and to apply them to another issue: aggression. You would only be asked this as an exam question if you had actually covered the topic of aggression in class. However, you might be asked this as a coursework essay question even if the lectures had not directly covered aggression. Your answer would demonstrate your ability to apply the nature–nurture debate to another area. For an essay question you would want to read up about the different theories of aggression in an introductory textbook (if you are a first-year student), or in books/ journals specifically on aggression (if you are a second- or third-year student).

   After a brief introduction, your essay should be divided into three sections. The first section would cover purely nativist explanations of aggression (e.g. that aggression is linked to the hormone testosterone or the Y chromosome, and that males are more aggressive because they evolved to be that way), and should then say what the problems with these explanations are. The second section would cover purely empiricist explanations of aggression (e.g. the social learning theory that children learn to be aggressive due to reinforcement from parents and peers, and/or due to modelling the behaviour of those they see around them or in the media). You should then discuss the limitations of these explanations. The third section should outline a possible interactionist explanation of aggression (e.g. that biological and genetic factors may predispose some people, particularly males, towards aggression, but that these factors could be exacerbated or counteracted by environmental factors such as social norms of behaviour, cultural notions of masculinity/femininity, deprivation, crowding, etc.). Your conclusion would probably accept the interactionist perspective (unless you can find overwhelming evidence for one of the other positions!). But you might want to also point out how there are many different ways in which 'nature' and 'nurture' can interact, and psychology's task is to investigate these further.

4. With this question you should first be clear about what is being asked. Remember that 'everyday psychology' is another way of saying 'common-sense understanding'. So this question is asking whether psychology should take account of people's common-sense understandings of human behaviour. Since the question uses the phrase 'everyday psychology', you should also use this phrase in your answer.

   You could answer this in three different ways. First, you could argue that psychology should not take account of everyday psychology because everyday psychology is very flawed and give reasons for this. Second, you could argue that psychology should take account of everyday psychology because otherwise it will not be useful and go through all the reasons for this. The best answers to this question would probably include a bit of both of these other answers, giving a balanced explanation of why psychology has neglected everyday psychology, and why it should perhaps pay it more attention. For a course-work essay, you would probably also want to read up on the social psychological research that has investigated everyday psychology as an issue in itself (e.g. attribution theory) and mention this. Remember to give a clear answer to the question in your conclusion, drawing on all the arguments you have put forward.

Section 6

Further reading and research

The issues of determinism, reductionism, mind–brain and nature–nurture are covered in more detail in several introductory textbooks. The following are helpful:

Gross, R. (1995) *Themes, Issues and Debates in Psychology.* London: Hodder & Stoughton.
Malim, T. and Birch, A. (1998) *Introductory Psychology.* London: Macmillan Press.

This shorter book also provides a briefer summary of determinism and the mind–brain debate.

Gross, R. and McIlveen, R. (1999) *Perspectives in Psychology.* London: Hodder & Stoughton.

This cartoon-style book is also very accessible:

Gellaty, A. and Zarate, O. (1998) *Mind and Brain for Beginners.* London: Icon Books.

For a lot more detail on problems with the 'nature' argument, see:

Rose, S., Lewontin, R. C. and Kamin, L. J. (1990) *Not in Our Genes: Biology, Ideology and Human Nature.* London: Penguin.

The issues around common sense and psychology are covered in a lot of depth in the chapter on 'everyday psychology' in:

Jones, D. and Elcock, J. (2001) *History and Theories of Psychology: A Critical Perspective.* London: Arnold.

Additional material about problems with common-sense understandings are included in:

Colman, A. M. (1999) *What Is Psychology?* London: Routledge.
Furnham, A. (2001) *All in the Mind: The Essence of Psychology.* London: Whurr Publishers.

Examination questions and answers

Chapter 1 Psychology and its history

Question
Claire is about to start a degree in psychology. When she tells her friend Sue about it Sue says 'Oh no, you'll start analysing me.' What should Claire say to put her friend at ease?

Answer
This is a question about what psychology is (see section 1 of Chapter 1). You occasionally get questions that are worded in this friendly style but it is important to remember that they still require a rigorous answer giving psychological examples.

The first thing to point out is the common error that Sue is making. She is confusing psychology with the related areas of psychiatry, psychotherapy and/or psychoanalysis. A good answer to this question would begin with an introduction explaining this error and how common it is. It could then have the following subsections:

1. Explain what psychology actually is, perhaps using Zimbardo's (1992) definition: 'the scientific study of the behaviour of individuals and their mental processes'. You could unpack this definition a bit to explain it and perhaps give some examples of psychological research and professional work (like the ones given in chapter 3).
2. Explain the confusion between psychology and psychiatry/psychotherapy. Explain that some psychologists are involved in using therapy with clients (clinical psychologists and counselling psychologists), but that most psychologists are concerned with 'normal' behaviour and study a number of people. An undergraduate like Claire certainly wouldn't be taught psychotherapeutic techniques. Also make clear that a psychiatrist has medical training and a psychotherapist or counsellor does not necessarily have a psychology degree.
3. Explain the confusion between psychology and psychoanalysis. Say that psychoanalysis is just one approach to psychology put forward by Freud. Explain that many of Freud's ideas have passed into common language, which is why people often think that is what psychology is, but that most modern psychologists dismiss Freud's theories.

You could also mention some popular depictions of psychology which might explain why Sue thinks all psychologists analyse people (e.g. Cracker, Frasier). A strong answer might also briefly consider psychological research and whether that can be said to be 'analysing people' (see Chapter 4). A very good answer would tackle the implications for this common view of psychology for psychologists working with people and carrying out research. Bringing it back to the specific question set you could conclude with what Claire should say to Sue, and perhaps why it is important to challenge such confused perceptions of psychology.

Question
Briefly outline the development of psychology since its emergence as a discipline in the late nineteenth century.

Answer

This is a more typical question from an introductory psychology exam. Be careful to read the question. You need to start with the emergence of psychology as a discipline and work forward to the present day. It would be very helpful to the reader to provide a brief time line to start with and then go through this expanding on the key events you have mentioned. This should include the following dates and events:

1879 – Wilhelm Wundt founds the first experimental laboratory in Leipzig, Germany.
1890 – William James publishes *Principles of Psychology* in the US.
1900 – Sigmund Freud publishes *The Interpretation of Dreams*, setting out his psychoanalytic theory.
1912 – Max Wertheimer publishes the earliest account of Gestalt psychology.
1913 – J. B. Watson publishes the article that launches behaviourism.
1951 – Carl Rogers publishes his *Client Centred Therapy*, a precursor to the founding of humanism.
1956 – the cognitive revolution.

If you can't remember the exact dates it is OK to put 'in the 1920s' or 'in the mid twentieth century'; similarly you could just say 'the book that sets out the X approach' rather than giving the book title.

A good answer to this question would briefly discuss the different contenders for the date of the 'emergence of psychology' and say that 1879 is the date that most psychologists agree on. A strong answer might consider why psychologists today might choose that as a date, considering the implications of the desire to see psychology as a science (see Chapter 4). The essay should then go through the events outlined above, discussing briefly the rise and fall of the different schools of psychology. Again, a very strong answer might consider issues such as the impact of the social context on the development (or not) or various schools (e.g. the Gestalt school and Nazism, humanism and the cultural context of the 1960s). It could also mention that the history of a discipline is written by the winners, and the implications of that for the concept of the cognitive revolution (which is generally accepted) and new paradigm psychology (which is not given much space in mainstream textbooks). You could conclude your essay with a brief paragraph about why it is useful for psychologists to be aware of this history (see Chapter 1).

Chapter 2 Theoretical approaches in psychology

Question

Outline the main characteristics of any one theory of learning.

Answer

In Chapter 2 we covered two main theories of learning: Pavlov's classical conditioning and Skinner's operant conditioning. You could choose either of these for your answer and explain it. Let's try Pavlov's theory since I always find that the easier one to remember.

Your answer should begin by explaining that the classical conditioning theory of learning held that learning occurs when we make an association between a neutral stimulus and a stimulus that reliably produces a response. You should then explain this with a specific example, Pavlov's dogs being the obvious one. This is where a picture really can be worth a thousand words. Remember this diagram from Chapter 2?

Draw this diagram and then explain how classical conditioning works in detail.

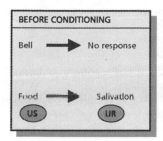 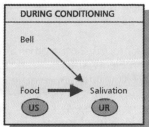 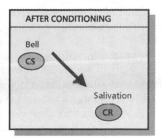

Classical conditioning

The question only asks you to outline the main characteristics of a theory of learning. However, if you have time and want to strengthen your answer you could also weigh up the strengths and weaknesses of this theory. A strength could be its explanation of how we learn phobias and its implications for how these may be treated. A weakness could be that it is limited and does not explain all learning. You could mention Skinner's operant conditioning as another form of learning, and more broadly how behaviourist theories neglect the involvement of mental processes in learning. You could mention Gestalt or cognitive theories of learning, like Köhler's 'insight learning' (see Chapter 1).

Question

Freud, Watson, Rogers and Broadbent are all contestants on *Big Brother*. They are voting to choose which one of them will be evicted next. They can all vote for one person, and the person with the most votes will be evicted. Say who you think will be evicted and why.

Answer

This is one of the hardest psychology questions I've ever seen, but something very similar was given to some friends of mine who are taking a psychology degree, so it is worth being prepared for. You are unlikely to get a question as tough as this, but reading this will mean that you will be ready for anything! This would definitely be an essay-type exam question, not a short-answer one. A short-answer version would be to ask for who just one of the contestants would vote.

The first step with any complex question like this is to unpack it. You need to ask yourself what it is really asking you to do. In this case, the question is really asking 'which of the approaches to psychology has least in common with the others?' The marker would want to see that you understood the major differences between the approaches and could use this knowledge to make a case for which approach is least like all the others.

A good way to structure your answer would be to take each person (and the approach that they come from) in turn. For each one you need to clearly state their approach, briefly say what it involves and then discuss what that approach would make of the other approaches, particularly any major points of agreement or disagreement. Figure 2.6 from Chapter 2 is extremely helpful here.

If you were confident enough, you could answer in the style of the question, imagining each of the theorists in the diary room and what they would say about the other contestants. Be careful though to make sure you get all the key points in.

For example, when you are discussing Broadbent you would say that he took the cognitive approach which models mental process using the information processing analogy of the brain. You could point out that, as a cognitivist, he would approve of Watson's behaviourist method of controlled experiments and disapprove of the case study techniques used by Freud and Rogers along with the subjective nature of their theories. When deciding who Broadbent would evict out of Freud and Rogers, you might point out that cognitivists share with humanists some uncertainty about pure determinism, and that

Rogers did make some attempt to study his techniques (Q sort). So you might conclude that Broadbent would choose Freud for eviction.

You need to go through the same process for the other three contestants. I would reckon that Watson would have similar problems with Freud and Rogers to Broadbent, but might particularly dislike Freud's completely unobservable notion of the unconscious. Freud would probably also choose Watson because of this difference. Rogers might choose either Watson or Freud for their deterministic notions of human beings. So it seems that Freud is the most likely to be evicted and Broadbent is most likely to win, having no votes at all.

A strong answer would consider the parallels between this hypothetical example and the history of psychology where the psychodynamic approach is rejected by most and cognitivism is now the dominant approach.

Chapter 3 Pure and applied psychology

Question
Describe any well-known pure psychological study. Indicate briefly any applied implications it might have.

Answer
For this question you could choose any of the pure crucial studies that we introduced in Chapter 3. For example, the Stroop test, Dement and Kleitman's (1957) study of sleep, Samuel and Bryant's (1984) study on Piaget's research into child development or Potter and Edward's (1990) discourse analysis study. This chapter describes all of these and gives some ideas about how they might be applied (e.g. the emotional Stroop task). You could apply the sleep research to help people with sleep disorders and Samuel and Bryant's research to helping children to learn in schools using appropriate teacher questioning. You could also use Pavlov's research as an example of pure research and discuss its clinical applications, as mentioned in the first question on Chapter 2 above.

Another good study to use for this question would be one of the cognitive example studies from Chapter 3: Loftus and Palmer's (1974) study on eyewitness testimony, since this is easy to remember and explain and has clear implications for legal psychology. Your answer should start by explaining that this is a classic study in pure psychology. Then it should outline the study, describing how Loftus and Palmer showed participants film-clips of traffic accidents and asked them about them using different wording. You should summarise the findings of the study: that participants estimated the speed of the cars as being faster if they were asked how fast they were going when they 'smashed into each other' rather than 'hit each other', and they were more likely to falsely remember that they saw broken glass in this former condition.

For the second part of the question, you should explain the importance of this research for legal psychology because it suggests that eyewitness testimony can be influenced by the questions asked. Juries should perhaps be made aware of this. A strong answer would briefly bring in further evidence that eyewitness testimonies are often flawed, but that juries place a great deal of emphasis on them even if they are shown to be flawed (see Harrower, 1998). You could also say how this study is relevant to clinical psychology since it shows that memories can be constructed by questioning. This has implications for the false memory syndrome debate (see section 4 of Chapter 3).

Question
Why do psychologists need to be aware of ethics when conducting research on human participants? What are the major ethical concepts that they should take into consideration?

Answer

This question requires that you introduce the area of ethics in psychology by explaining why psychologists need to be ethical in their research, and then go on to outline the major ethical considerations.

You should point out that, as well as the moral responsibility to protect the rights and dignity of participants, psychologists need to treat them well in order to ensure that people will take part in psychological studies. Without human participants there would be no psychology.

For the major ethical considerations you should give the BPS ethical guidelines. Remember that these included the following:

- informed consent being given by participants;
- deception being avoided unless absolutely necessary;
- participants being debriefed after the study, being told its true nature and offered support if necessary;
- participants being able to withdraw from the investigation at any time;
- confidentiality and anonymity being maintained;
- protection of participants from physical or emotional harm.

You could describe each of these in a bit more depth, considering some of the difficulties in ensuring that they are met. A strong answer might go even further to discuss the tensions between conducting research that is ethical and ensuring that it is objective and valid (see Chapter 4). You could also mention the power of the researcher and the problems this can pose for ethical research (whether participants can really give informed consent, and the potential impact of research on social policy).

Chapter 4 Themes and debates in psychological research

Question
Discuss the factors that may distort the outcome of scientific investigations.

Answer
You should recognise that this question relates to section 3 of Chapter 4: the impact of the research situation. It is asking for the factors that can adversely influence the outcome of psychological studies.

The initial paragraphs of your answer to this question should introduce the importance of objectivity in psychological research, explaining that most psychologists aim to be scientific and objective, meaning that they attempt to measure things accurately without being influenced by personal feelings or opinions. There are some difficulties with psychology being objective since it involves human beings studying other human beings. You should then say that the rest of the essay will go through some of the main factors that may distort the outcome of scientific investigations, causing problems for objectivity and particularly external validity (whether the findings of the study can be generalised to the 'real world'). Some of these factors are:

- **experimenter bias and effects** – the influence of the culture, gender or historical time the experimenter is living in. The experimenter may also subtly give away the nature of the hypothesis to participants;
- **demand characteristics** – features of the study that make participants behave in abnormal ways. Mention Orne's (1962) findings about the extreme things people would do in experiments that they would not do in normal life;

127

- **volunteer characteristics** – differences between the type of people who volunteer for psychological studies and the type of people who do not. Volunteers are more easily influenced and neurotic (Ora, 1965). They are also frequently undergraduate students and therefore not representative of the population as a whole;
- **participants trying to work out the experimental hypothesis** – either to conform to it, mess it up, be defensive or try to be as normal as possible;
- **social desirability and the Hawthorn effect** – participants may try to be seen in a positive light and may act differently because they are being observed.

In your conclusion you could reiterate that these factors all threaten external validity, which makes it difficult to say that the results of studies are useful. A strong answer would consider the ways in which psychologists have responded to this problem. Some have tried to increase objectivity by using double blind procedures, random sampling, etc. Others have stopped trying to be scientific and have moved towards more qualitative ways of studying people.

Question
Discuss the problems that researchers face when trying to measure psychological phenomena such as intelligence, attitudes and personality.

Answer
This question is about bias in psychological research (section 2 of Chapter 3). You need to consider ethnocentrism (the fact that psychology is steeped in western values), androcentrism (most psychological theorists and researchers come from a male perspective) and historical bias (the issue that the time in which studies are conducted and theories proposed influences these studies and theories).

Because the question explicitly mentions intelligence, attitudes and personality, it would be good to bring all these into your answer. You should start by introducing each of the types of bias briefly, and then devote a section of your answer to each in detail. In the 'ethnocentrism' section you might want to mention past assumptions about racial differences in intelligence and personality. In the 'androdrocentrism' section, you could talk about research suggesting that women have more 'conforming' personalities, and the fact that such research was later found to be flawed since it used tasks that men were more familiar with (Sistrunk and McDavid, 1971). In the section on historical bias, you could talk about the 'authoritarian' attitude and the historical variation in whether this is seen as a meaningful concept at all and whether it is regarded as a positive or negative thing.

You could conclude by examining the difficulties inherent in trying to put numbers to complex psychological phenomena like intelligence, personality and attitudes. Personal and cultural values impact on whether we see such concepts as existing and important, whether we measure them, how we value them and whether we look for gender, racial or other differences on these measures.

As with the previous question, a strong answer might consider the different ways in which psychologists have responded to such issues of bias. Again, some have attempted to make their psychology more objective, while others have embraced reflexivity: trying to be aware of their biases and positions and how these might influence their work.

Chapter 5 Themes and debates in psychological theory

Question
What are the strengths and weaknesses of a reductionist approach to psychology?

Answer

The introduction to your answer to this question should give a brief definition of reductionism, explaining that it is the argument that phenomena are nothing but their constituent parts and that human behaviours can be best explained by breaking them down into these parts. You could give a brief example or two of how these work (e.g. behaviourists explain behaviour in terms of learnt links between stimuli and responses, evolutionary psychologists in terms of genes).

The rest of the question is answered in section 2 of Chapter 5 and summarised in Figure 5.4. Displaying the strengths and weaknesses in a table like the one below is a very clear way of laying it out. You can then go through each argument in more depth giving examples, as in Chapter 5.

Strengths and weaknesses of the reductionist approach

Strengths	Weaknesses
Fits with psychology's aim to be a science.	No need for psychology if all behaviour explained at lower levels.
Some psychological questions are best answered at lower levels.	Some psychological questions are not well answered at lower levels.
Gives simple, concise explanations for psychological phenomena.	Reductionist arguments overlook other levels of explanation, producing limited understanding of behaviour.
Can suggest successful interventions.	Reductionism doesn't take account of 'emergent properties'.
	Reductionist explanations have been sought for particular reasons or political purposes with negative consequences.

If you have time you might also want to explain the two most common types of reductionism in psychology (physiological and biological reductionism), and the branches of psychology that are less reductionist (e.g. Gestalt and social psychology). A strong answer would relate this question to the nature–nurture debate and some of the problems inherent in looking for purely biological explanations for human behaviour.

Question

Briefly outline the debate between environmental and hereditarian explanations of human psychology.

Answer

This is a very common question to be asked on a psychology course. The nature–nurture (or environmental–hereditarian) debate is discussed a lot and runs through various different areas of psychology. You might well be asked such a question specifically in relation to language acquisition, personality, aggression or some other aspect of human behaviour.

This question is more general, however. You can use the aspects of human behaviour mentioned above as concrete examples in your answer, but you shouldn't just focus on one of them to the exclusion of the others.

It is important to acknowledge in your introduction that very few psychologists take a completely environmental or hereditarian position. Most are interactionist to some degree. You should also describe these three positions clearly. The strong environmental position holds that new-born children are blank slates whose psychological characteristics are shaped by their environment. The strong hereditarian position is that babies carry innate blueprints that determine their psychological characteristics.

A good way to structure your answer would be to start with one of the extreme positions, giving examples where it seems to work and some where it doesn't. Then move on to the other position and do the same. Finally, explain the interactionist position with a couple of examples to demonstrate the relationship between inherited and environmental factors.

For example, you might start with the heriditarian position and explain how some physical characteristics and illnesses seem to be inherited. Chomsky proposed that the 'language acquisition device' was also inherited, since children everywhere acquire language at around the same age. But psychological characteristics are not so simple to explain. For example, there is evidence that parents modify their language to help children learn and children learn the social function of language through their environment.

Moving on to the environmental position, you could give the example of a phobia as something that seems to be learned (see Chapter 2). However, you could point out the problems in assuming that such psychological characteristics are completely learnt by showing that some characteristics seem to be present from a very young age, such as boys being more active than girls. Also, there is twin study evidence for some genetic component to characteristics like intelligence.

Gendered behaviour is a very good example to give for the interactionist perspective. Remember Ruble's (1988) summary of how genetic differences between male and female babies might predispose them to act in gendered ways, but that their treatment by their parents, along with cultural factors, might exacerbate these differences.

Your likely conclusion to this essay would be that an interactionist approach is more appropriate to human psychology than either the extreme environmental or hereditarian explanations. A strong answer would also explain that it is problematic to try to determine how much behaviour is determined by each factor (genetics and the environment) because the different factors combine in complex ways. A better question for psychology to ask is how genetic factors interact with the environment.

Further reading

These are some books that you might want to look at to expand your knowledge and understanding of the issues and topics covered in this book.

Some good (but large) comprehensive introductory textbooks are:

Eysenck, M. (ed.) (1998) *Psychology: An Integrated Approach.* Harlow: Longman.
Eysenck, M. (2000) *Psychology: A Student's Handbook.* Hove: Psychology Press.
Gross, R. (1992) *Psychology: The Science of Mind and Behaviour.* London: Hodder & Stoughton.
Hayes, N. (1994) *Foundations of Psychology: An Introductory Text.* London: Routledge.
Malim, T. and Birch, A. (1998) *Introductory Psychology.* London: Macmillan Press.

Some smaller texts that cover some of the themes from this book are:

Benson, N. C. and Grove, S. (1999) *Introducing Psychology.* London: Icon.
Butler, G. and McManus, F. (1998) *Psychology: A Very Short Introduction.* Oxford: Oxford University Press.
Colman, A. M. (1995) *What is Psychology?* London: Routledge.
Gross, R. (1995) *Themes, Issues and Debates in Psychology.* London: Hodder & Stoughton.
Gross, R. and McIlveen, R. (1999) *Perspectives in Psychology.* London: Hodder & Stoughton.
Hayes, N. (1994) *Teach Yourself Psychology*. London: Hodder & Stoughton.

Details about most of the crucial studies mentioned in this book can be found in:

Banyard, P. and Grayson, A. (2000) *Introducing Psychological Research.* Basingstoke: Palgrave.

A very helpful book on psychology study skills with lots of exercises is:

Collins, S. C. and Kneale, P. E. (2001) *Study Skills For Psychology Students: A Practical Guide.* London: Arnold.

Some more challenging books that take the issues in this book further include the following:

Ashworth, P. (2000) *Psychology and 'Human Nature'.* Hove: Psychology Press.
Howitt, D. (1991) *Concerning Psychology: Psychology Applied to Social Issues.* Buckingham: Open University Press.
Jones, D. and Elcock, J. (2001) *History and Theories of Psychology: A Critical Perspective.* London: Arnold.
Richards, G. (1996) *Putting Psychology in its Place: An Introduction from a Critical Historical Perspective.* London: Routledge.

I'd also strongly recommend reading *The Psychologist* magazine, which comes out each month, and checking out the BPS website at *www.bps.org.uk.*

If you decide to go further with your psychology studies and take courses in the various different areas of psychology outlined in Chapter 3, you will find other Crucial Study Texts in this series very useful. The Crucial Study Text on research methods and statistics is an excellent companion to this book for those taking a whole psychology degree.

References

Adler, A. (1927) *The Practice and Theory of Individual Psychology*. New York: Harcourt Brace Jovanovich.

Anderson, N. and Shackleton, V. (1993) *Successful Selection Interviewing*. Oxford: Blackwell Publishers.

Asch, S. E. (1955) 'Opinions and social pressure', *Scientific American*, 193: 31–5.

Ashworth, P. (2000) *Psychology and 'Human Nature'*. Hove: Psychology Press.

Axline, Virginia M. (1990) *Dibs: In Search of Self*. London: Penguin Books.

Bandura, A. (1977) *Social Learning Theory*. Englewood Cliffs, NJ: Prentice-Hall (included in Banyard and Grayson, 2000).

Banyard, P. (1996) *Applying Psychology to Health*. London: Hodder & Stoughton.

Banyard, P. and Grayson, A. (2000) *Introducing Psychological Research*. Basingstoke: Palgrave.

Baumeister, R. F. (1997) *Evil: Inside Human Cruelty and Violence*. New York: W. H. Freeman.

Beale, D., Cox, T., Clarke, D., Lawrence, C. and Leather, P. (1998) Temporal architecture of violent incidents, *Journal of Occupational Health Psychology*, 3 (1): 65–82.

Benson, N. C. and Grove, S. (1999) *Introducing Psychology*, London: Icon.

Birch, H. (1993) *Moving Targets: Women, Murder and Representation*. London: Virago Press.

Bouchard, T. and McGuire, M. (1981) 'Familial studies of intelligence: a review', *Science*, 212: 1055–9.

Britton, P. (1997) *The Jigsaw Man*. London: Bantam Press.

Broadbent, D. E. (1981) 'Non-corporeal explanations in psychology', in Heath, A. F. (ed.), *Scientific Explanation*. Oxford: Clarendon Press.

Burr, V. (1995) *An Introduction to Social Constructionism*. London: Routledge.

Burr, V. (1998) *Gender and Social Psychology*. London: Routledge.

Butler, G. and McManus, F. (1998) *Psychology: A Very Short Introduction*. Oxford: Oxford University Press.

Byrne, W. (1994) 'The biological evidence challenged', *Scientific American*, May, 26–31.

Canter, D. (1994) *Criminal Shadows*. London. HarperCollins.

Cardwell, M. (1999) *Ethical Issues in Psychology*. London: Routledge.

Cherry, E. C. (1953) 'Some experiments on the recognition of speech with one and two ears', *Journal of Acoustical Society of America*, 25: 975–9.

Clarke, D. D. (1987) 'Fundamental problems with fundamental research: a meta-theory for social psychology', *Philosophica*, 40: 23–61.

Collins, S. C. and Kneale, P. E. (2001) *Study Skills For Psychology Students: A Practical Guide*. London: Arnold.

Colman, A. M. (1999) *What is Psychology?* London: Routledge.

Conway, M. A. (1997) *Recovered Memories and False Memories*. Oxford: Oxford University Press.

Coolican, H., Cassidy, T., Chercher, A., Harrower, J., Penny, G., Sharp, R., Walley, M. and Westbury, T. (1996), *Applied Psychology*. London: Hodder & Stoughton.

Craik, F. I. M. and Lockhart, R. S. (1972) 'Levels of processing: a framework for memory research', *Journal of Verbal Learning and Verbal Behaviour*, 11: 671–84. (included in Banyard and Grayson, 2000).

Crick, F. (1994) *The Astonishing Hypothesis: The Scientific Search for the Soul*. London: Simon & Schuster.

Dement, W. and Kleitmann, N. (1957) 'The relation of eye movements during sleep to dream activity: an objective method for the study of dreaming', *Journal of Experimental Psychology*, 53 (5): 339–46 (included in Banyard and Grayson, 2000).

Erikson, E. H. (1950) *Childhood and Society*. New York: Norton.

Eysenck, H. J. (1957) *Sense and Nonsense in Psychology*. London: Penguin.

Eysenck, H. J. (1985) *Decline and Fall of the Freudian Empire*. London: Penguin.

Eysenck, M. (ed.) (1998) *Psychology: An Integrated Approach*. Harlow: Longman.

Eysenck, M. (2000) *Psychology: A Student's Handbook*. Hove: Psychology Press.

Festinger, L., Pepitone, A. and Newcombe, T. (1952) 'Some consequences of deindividuation in a group', *Journal of Abnormal and Social Psychology*, 47: 382–9.

Freud, S. (1909) 'Analysis of a phobia of a five-year-old boy', in the Pelican Freud Library (1977), Vol. 8, Case Histories 1, 169–306. (included in Banyard and Grayson, 2000).

Furnham, A. (2001) *All in the Mind: The Essence of Psychology*. London: Whurr Publishers.

Gale, A. (1994) 'Futures for Applied Psychology', in Spurgeon, P., Davies, R. and Chapman, T. (eds), *Elements of Applied Psychology*, Chur, Switzerland: Harwood Academic.

Garnham, A. (1991) *The Mind in Action*. London: Routledge.

Gellaty, A. and Zarate, O. (1998), *Mind and Brain for Beginners*. London: Icon Books.

Gilligan, C. and Attanucci, J. (1988) 'Two moral orientations: gender differences and similarities', *Merrill-Palmer Quarterly*, 34: 223–37 (included in Banyard and Grayson, 2000).

Gould, S. J. (1981) *The Mismeasure of Man*. London: Penguin.

Gould, S. J. (1982) 'A nation of morons', *New Scientist*, 6 May, 349–52 (included in Banyard and Grayson, 2000).

Graham, H. (1986) *The Human Face of Psychology: Humanistic Psychology in Its Historical, Social and Cultural Context*, Buckingham: Open University Press.

Gross, R. (1992) *Psychology: The Science of Mind and Behaviour*. London: Hodder & Stoughton.

Gross, R. (1995) *Themes, Issues and Debates in Psychology*. London: Hodder & Stoughton.

Gross, R. (1999) *Key Studies in Psychology*. London: Hodder & Stoughton.

Gross, R. and McIlveen, R. (1999) *Perspectives in Psychology*. London: Hodder & Stoughton.

Haney, C., Banks, C. and Zimbardo, P. (1973) 'A study of prisoners and guards in a simulated prison', *Naval Research Reviews*, 30 (9): 4–17 (included in Banyard and Grayson, 2000).

Harré, R. and Secord, P. F. (1972) *The Explanation of Social Behaviour*. Oxford: Blackwell.

Harrower, J. (1998) *Applying Psychology to Crime*. London: Hodder & Stoughton.

Hartley, J. and Branthwaite, A. (1999) *The Applied Psychologist*. Buckingham: Open University Press.

Hayes, N. (1994) *Foundations of Psychology: An Introductory Text*. London: Routledge.

Hayes, N. (1999) *Teach Yourself Psychology*. London: Hodder & Stoughton.

Hayes, N. and Stratton, P. (1999) *A Student's Dictionary of Psychology*. London: Arnold.

Hayward, S. (1996) *Applying Psychology to Organisations*. London: Hodder & Stoughton.

Heffernan, T. M. (1997) *A Student's Guide to Studying Psychology*. Hove: Psychology Press.

Hogg, M. A. and Vaughan, G. M. (2002) *Social Psychology*. Harlow: Prentice Hall.

Horne, J. A. (2001) 'State of the art: Sleep', *The Psychologist*, 14 (6): 302–6.

Houston, J. P. (1983) 'Psychology: a closed system of self-evident information?' *Psychological Reports*, 52 (1): 203–8.

Howitt, D. (1991) *Concerning Psychology: Psychology Applied to Social Issues*. Buckingham: Open University Press.

Howitt, D. and Owasu-Bempah, J. (1994) *The Racism of Psychology*. London: Harvester Wheatsheaf.

Hyman, R. (1977) 'Cold reading: how to convince strangers that you know all about them', *The Zetetic*, 1: 18–37.

James, W. (1890) *Principles of Psychology*. New York: Henry Holt.

Jones, D. and Elcock, J. (2001) *History and Theories of Psychology: A Critical Perspective*. London: Arnold.

Jones, S. (1993) *The Language of the Genes*. London: Flamingo.

Jung, C. G. (1964) *Man and His Symbols*. London: Aldus-Jupiter Books.

Kimmel, A. J. (1996) *Ethical Issues in Behavioural Research*. Oxford: Blackwell.

Kirkman, J. (1993) *Full Marks: Advice on Punctuation for Scientific and Technical Writing*. Malborough: Ramsbury Books.

Kitzinger, C., Coyle A., Wilkinson, S. and Milton, M. (1998) 'Towards lesbian and gay psychology', *The Psychologist*, November, 529–33.

Kohlberg, L. (1968) 'The child as a moral philosopher', *Psychology Today,* 2: 25–30 (included in Banyard and Grayson, 2000).

Kozlowski, L. T. and Cutting, J. E. (1977) 'Recognising the sex of a walker from a dynamic point-light display', *Perception and Psychophysics,* 21: 575–80 (included in Banyard and Grayson, 2000).

Krupat, E. and Garonzik, R. (1994) 'Subjects' expectations and the search for alternatives to deception in social psychology', *British Journal of Social Psychology*, 33: 211–22.

La Berge, D. (1975) 'Acquisition of automatic processing in perceptual and associative learning', in Radditt, P. M. A. and Dormic, S. (eds) *Attention and Performance*, Vol. 5. London: Academic Press.

Lang, P. J. and Lazovik, A. D. (1963) 'Experimental desensitisation of a phobia', *Journal of Abnormal and Social Psychology*, 66: 519–25 (included in Banyard and Grayson, 2000).

Lea, S. E. F. (2000) 'Towards an ethical use of animals', *The Psychologist*, 13, (11): 556–7.

Leather, P. and Lawrence, C. (1995) 'Perceiving pub violence: the symbolic influence of social and environmental factors', *British Journal of Social Psychology*, 34: 395–407.

Lenneberg, E. H. (1967) *Biological Foundations of Language*. New York: Wiley.

LeVay, S. and Hamer, D. H. (1994) 'Evidence for a biological influence in male homosexuality', *Scientific American*, May, 20–5.

Lindsay, G. and Lunt, I. (1993) 'The challenge of change', *The Psychologist,* 6 (5): 210–13.

Loftus, E. F. and Palmer, J. C. (1974) 'Reconstruction of automobile destruction: An example of the interaction between language and memory', *Journal of Verbal Learning and Verbal Behaviour*, 13: 585–9 (included in Banyard and Grayson, 2000).

Malim, T. and Birch, A. (1998) *Introductory Psychology*. London: Macmillan Press.

Matthews, A. and MacLeod, C. (1985) 'Selective processing of threat cues in anxiety states', *Behaviour Research and Therapy*, 23: 563–9.

Milgram, S. (1963) 'Behavioural study of obedience', *Journal of Abnormal and Social Psychology*, 67: 371–8 (included in Banyard and Grayson, 2000).

Morgan, M. (1996) 'Qualitative research: a package deal?', *The Psychologist*, January, 31–2.

Moscovici, S. and Zavalloni, M. (1969) 'The group as a polarizer of attitudes', *Journal of Personality and Social Psychology*, 12: 125–35.

Newell, A. and Simon, H. A. (1972) *Human Problem Solving*. Englewood Cliffs, NJ: Prentice Hall.

Nisbett, R. E. and Wilson, T. D. (1977) 'Telling more than we can know: verbal reports on mental processes', *Psychological Review*, 84: 231–359.

Ora, J. P. (1965) *Characteristics of the volunteer for psychological investigation*. Office of Naval Research Contract 2149 (03), Technical Report 27.

Orne, M. T. (1962) 'On the social psychology of the psychological experiment – with particular reference to demand characteristics', *American Psychologist*, 17 (11): 776–83 (included in Banyard and Grayson, 2000).

Pease, A. and Pease, B. (1999) *Why Men Don't Listen and Women Can't Read Maps*. London: Orion.

Penfield, W. (1947) 'Some observations on the cerebral cortex of man', *Proceedings of the Royal Society*, 134, 349.

Pennebaker, J. W. (1997) *Opening Up: The Healing Power of Expressing Emotions*. London: Guilford Press.

Popper, K. (1959) *The Logic of Scientific Discovery*. London: Hutchinson.

Potter, J. and Edwards, D. (1990) 'Nigel Lawson's tent: Discourse analysis, attribution theory and the social psychology of fact', *European Journal of Social Psychology*, 20: 405–24 (included in Banyard and Grayson, 2000).

The Psychologist (1998) 'Quantitative vs. qualitative debate', November, 481–9.

The Psychologist (2001) 'Freud special issue', December.

The Psychologist (2002) 'Media Ethics Consultation', July, 15 (7): 342–5.

Richards, G. (1996) *Putting Psychology in Its Place: An Introduction from a Critical Historical Perspective*. London: Routledge.

Rose, S., Lewontin, R. C. and Kamin, L. J. (1990) *Not in Our Genes: Biology, Ideology and Human Nature*. London: Penguin.

Rosenhan, D. L. (1973) 'On being sane in insane places', *Science*, 179: 250–8. (included in Banyard and Grayson, 2000).

Rosenthal, R. and Fode, K. L. (1963) 'The effects of experimenter bias on the performance of the albino rat', *Behavioural Science*, 8: 183–9.

Rosenthal, R. and Jacobson, L. (1966) 'Teachers' expectancies: determinants of pupils' I.Q. gains', *Psychological Reports*, 19: 115–18 (included in Banyard and Grayson, 2000).

Ruble, D. N. (1988) 'Sex role development', in Bornstien, M. H. and Lamb, M. E. (eds), *Social, Emotional and Personality Development. Part III of Developmental Psychology: An Advanced Textbook*. Hove: Lawrence Erlbaum Associates.

Russell, S. (1993) *Grammar, Structure and Style*. Oxford: Oxford University Press.

Rutter, M. and Rutter, M. (1993) *Developing Minds: Challenge and Continuity Across the Lifespan*. London: Penguin.

Samuel, J. and Bryant, P. (1984) 'Asking only one question in the conservation experiment', *Journal of Child Psychology and Psychiatry*, 25: 315–18 (included in Banyard and Grayson, 2000).

Scarr, S. (1992) 'Developmental theories for the 1990s: development and individual differences', *Child Development*, 63: 1–19.

Scarr, S. and Weinberg, R. (1976) 'IQ performance of black children adopted by white families', *American Psychologist*, 31: 726–39.

Searle, J. R. (1980) 'Minds, brains and programs', *Behavioural and Brain Sciences*, 3: 417–57 (included in Banyard and Grayson, 2000).

Sherif, M. (1956) 'Experiments in group conflict', *Scientific American*, 195: 54–8 (included in Banyard and Grayson, 2000).

Shermer, M. (1997) *Why People Believe Weird Things*. New York: Freeman.

Sherrard, Carol (1997) 'Never mind the bathwater, keep hold of the baby: qualitative research', *The Psychologist*, April, 161–2.

Sistrunk, F. and McDavid, J. W. (1971) 'Sex variable in conforming behaviour', *Journal of Personality and Social Psychology*, 2: 200–7.

Skinner, B. F. (1948) *Walden Two*. New York: Macmillan.

Smith, M. L. and Glass, G. V. (1977) 'Meta-analysis of psychotherapy outcome studies', *American Psychologist*, 32: 752–60 (included in Banyard and Grayson, 2000).

Smith, P. B. and Bond, M. H. (1993) *Social Psychology Across Cultures: Analysis and Perspectives*. London: Harvester Wheatsheaf.

Stevens, R. (1995) 'Freudian theories of personality', in Hampson, S. E. and Colman, A. M. (eds), *Individual Differences and Personality*. Harlow: Longman.

Stevenson, C. and Cooper, N. (1997) 'Qualitative and quantitative research', *The Psychologist*, April, 159–60.

Stratton, P. and Hayes, N. (1999) *A Student's Dictionary of Psychology* . London: Arnold.

Stroop, J. R. (1935) 'Studies of interference in serial verbal reactions', *Journal of Experimental Psychology*, 18: 643–62.

Tedeshi, J. T., Lindskold, S. and Rosenfield, P. (1985), *Introduction to Social Psychology*. New York: West.

Thomas, J. C. (1974) 'An analysis of behaviour in the hobbits–orcs problem', *Cognitive Psychology*, 6: 257–69.

Watson, J. B. and Rayner, R. (1920) 'Conditioned emotional reactions', *Journal of Experimental Psychology*, 3: 1–14 (included in Banyard and Grayson, 2000).

Will, J. A., Self, P. A. and Datan, N. (1976) 'Maternal behaviour and perceived sex of infant', *American Journal of Orthopsychiatry*, 46: 135–9.

Woods, B. (1998) *Applying Psychology to Sport*. London: Hodder & Stoughton.

Valentine, E. R. (1992) *Conceptual Issues in Psychology*. London: Routledge.

Zimbardo, P. G. (1992) *Psychology and Life*. New York: HarperCollins.

Index